TEACHING THE DYSLEXIC CHILD

ANITA N. GRIFFITHS EdD

ACADEMIC THERAPY PUBLICATIONS
Novato, California

Copyright © 1978, by Academic Therapy Publications, Inc. All rights reserved. Printed in the United States of America. No part of this publication may be reproduced, stored in a retrieval system, or transmitted, in any form or by any means, electronic, mechanical photocopying, recording, or otherwise, without the prior written permission of the publisher.

Academic Therapy Publications
28 Commercial Boulevard
Novato, California 94947

Books, tests, and materials for and about the learning disabled

International Standard Book Number: 0-87879-205-8

    7   6
  0 9 8 7 6 5 4 3

Library of Congress Cataloging in Publication Data

Griffiths, Anita N
   Teaching the dyslexic child.

   Bibliography: p.
   1. Dyslexia. 2. Reading--Remedial teaching.
I. Title.
LB1050.5.G72   371.9'14   78-12875
ISBN 0-87879-205-8

Table of Contents

PROLOGUE

PART ONE — WHAT IS DYSLEXIA?

- 13   Do You Believe?
- 17   What Is Dyslexia?
- 23   What Dyslexia Looks Like to the Parent
- 27   Myths About Learning
  Or Things We Have Always Known
  About Learning That Are Not True
- 33   Self Concept and Learning
- 39   Learning About the Brain
- 45   Reading and Writing are Important
- 49   Junior and the Need to Learn

PART TWO — TEACHING DYSLEXIC CHILDREN

- 57   How Do You Teach A Dyslexic To Read?
- 61   What I Have Seen Others Do
- 65   The First Hour
- 71   One Lesson
- 75   How I Teach the Writing of Letters and Words
- 81   What Can Children Write About?
- 87   You Are The Expert
- 97   How You Can Help

EPILOGUE

BIBLIOGRAPHY

- 123   What Dyslexia Looks Like to the Teacher

To Jimmy

PROLOGUE

Why should I want to write this book? The shelves are growing heavy with books about dyslexia—how to diagnose it and how to remediate the condition when it is found. I am never more relaxed and effective than when I am engrossed in the learning process with another person and I do not lack for applicants. I no longer stand in need of a list of publications with which to impress a potential employer. Do I write in the hope of more money? The answer has to be in the negative, for I have never been able to feel that the money in my bank account is related in any way to the work I do. When the fact is brought home to me I receive it with embarrassment, for I feel vaguely guilty about being paid for something that is fun. I like the money to be there so that I can do the things which are important to me, but I feel uncomfortable about the fact that it is there because of something I do for children.

Then why am I writing this book? It is not to summarize all the deep wisdom I possess, nor is it really to try to convince others that they should follow in my footsteps. We are getting close to my feelings, now. For all of my adult life I have been engaged in a search. I have not always known what I am searching for, but I have never doubted that I am searching. As in the childhood game of "hot and cold," I know when I am "cold," for the enthusiasm leaves me, and I leave that job with no thought of the financial sacrifice involved. I know when I am getting "warm" for the hairs on my arms and on the back of my neck stand up.

There is no one kind of experience which calls up this reaction. I felt it when I stood in front of Michelangelo's *David*, and I felt it when I first heard Horowitz play *Chopin*, and I felt it when I went hang-gliding. Somehow, these are fringe benefits, though, for they come unexpectedly. Throughout my mature life there has been some sort of steady, life-giving source of joy and delight. It is almost always present when I am working and sharing with children, but it is not limited to the presence of children, for the surge is often present when I am interacting with adults, and it may come when I am totally alone.

The key to each of these symphonies of the soul is that I feel that I am coming always closer to finding out something which is still hidden from my gaze. Why are we the way we are? Sometimes I have a flash of insight about how my own brain works. That soggy mass which looks as if it could have no more use than a damp sponge is, evidently, where I really live, where I develop compassion, where I open and close the windows of my life, and where I learn to love and hate. When I sat upon a stage with wires hooked to my hands and learned that, by biofeedback, I could cause my hands to become alternately warm and cold, I was astounded. My brain could, at my command, control my bodily temperature. But when I think "my command" I have to mean the command of my brain, for I exist only as my brain exists.

More often than personal insight, I have stirring experiences of empathy when I am with a child, and am able to get a small glimpse of how that child learns. I am sometimes suffused by a surge of love. Sometimes I feel that I have been given a peek at that child's inner being.

A short time ago, I had a conversation with a ten-year-old boy. He explained to me, quite seriously, that there were two reasons for not being able to read. "One is being stupid, and the other is being lazy," he reasoned. Since he could not read at all, and since he knew very well he was not lazy, it followed that he was stupid. "Wanna see me run? Wanna see me clean up this whole building? Wanna see me fight a big, humongus alligator? Wanna see me mow grass for three hours? If you do, I'll show you I ain't lazy. So how you gonna teach me to read?"

I simply sat there, looking into his angry, hurt face, and I ached all over. He glared back at me for a few seconds, and then rescued me with, "Guess it won't hurt none to try."

I have walked this path many times, but for an instant I am afraid. I am not allowed six months to plug away. I cannot rely upon a workbook. *I* am the workbook, and my pages must be magic ones. I really have one chance, and I cannot postpone it. Time is my enemy, for I have only 55 minutes. But time is my ally, too, for Bart knows that something important must happen between us. I can feel him gathering his senses into concentration. What if I can't bridge the gap that stands between Bart and the understanding he must have? What if no electricity snaps between Bart's brain and the symbols on a page?

An hour later, it has happened! I am jubilant; Bart looks stunned. He knows he is beginning to read. All the wonderful world of books is within his grasp. He looks at me with a level gaze and asks, "How did I do that? What did I do?" He is, of course, quite right in saying that *he* did something, not that I did it.

My answer is inadequate: "I don't know. I wish I did. I think I can help you do some more of whatever it was that you did." At that, Bart gives me a look of pure delight and trust, and the hairs on my arm stand up.

I really do not know what happened. But I was there when the glory happened, and I shall never be quite the same. I shall remain in debt to Bart, and I shall continue to search. That is it; I am still searching. That is what this book is all about.

PART ONE

What Is Dyslexia?

. . . I struggled through the alphabet as if it had been a bramble-bush, getting considerably worried and scratched by every letter. After that, I fell among those thieves, the nine figures, who seemed every evening to do something new to disguise themselves and baffle recognition. But at last I began, in a purblind groping way, to read, write and cipher, on the very smallest scale.

Great Expectations

CHARLES DICKENS

Do You Believe?

Dyslexia[2] : That awful word is taboo in many school systems, and some educators recoil visibly and verbally when they hear the word. What is it about this word that causes negative, emotional responses from some people who deal with children? The use of the word by one of us who works with these handicapped children may bring on the vehement response, "I do *not* believe in dyslexia!"

Such a statement is often troubling to a parent or to others who are trying to help a dyslexic child compensate for his handicap. Perhaps we should examine the word and its effects in as dispassionate a way as possible. We cannot lump all these non-believers into a convenient category and think of them as "the bad guys," for it takes only a little thought to realize that they are, often, very "good guys."

What *is* the problem? We *must* be interested in the problem, for our dyslexic children are going to be meeting and interacting with these adults. I have asked the people who were adults when I was a child why the word *cancer* was whispered, not spoken. Very little was known about cancer, and it was a frightening thing to watch someone die from a disease which no one understood. If the word was never spoken, it could never be "leaked" to people outside the family; for if it were known, it might well be felt that it was due to "bad blood," and no one would want to marry a young woman or a young man from a home with bad blood!

The key word to describe this reaction is *fear*. Surely, no one in this enlightened time can be afraid of the word *dyslexia*? But that is exactly what causes the recoil. Surely, no one can think that it is caused by "bad blood"? We do not use those outdated words, but the condition is apparently inherited, and does "run in families." Perhaps we are a little more open-minded today about handicaps, but many people equate reading ability with intelligence, and are you sure you would want your daughter to marry someone who cannot read?

There are probably many other reasons for finding this word offensive. We cannot look at a dyslexic cell under the microscope, and we cannot give medication to cure it.

When we speak about how a child is affected and what causes him to act as he does, it is necessary to speak of the brain, and the way the brain processes information. As soon as the brain enters into the discussion many people jump to the conclusion that if the brain is affected the child cannot learn very much. *Retarded* or *brain-damaged* is the next thought, and these two words have not yet outgrown their stigma. People still ask the parents of brain-damaged children which side of the family is to blame for retardation, and if they would be afraid to have another child.

There is yet another factor which affects educators. When many of our educators went to college there were no classes in which dyslexia was discussed. One elementary school principal said to me, "There was no dyslexia when I was a child, and none when I went to college. If it had existed, there certainly would have been some mention of it in some of my course work. If there was none then, how can there be so much of it today?" He is one of the people who does not "believe in dyslexia." Of course it wasn't taught, because it is only in the last ten to fifteen years that the condition has been recognized and described. There is one sure-fire way to make a believer out of a non-believer. I have never known an educator to remain skeptical when it turns out that his or her own child is afflicted.

But where *were* these children a generation ago? Of course they were here, but were just not diagnosed. Or, perhaps they *were* diagnosed, but incorrectly, for their files were full of notations such as:

"immature"
"unmotivated"
"lack of parental interest"
"lazy"
"short attention span"
"lack of ability to concentrate"

There is also another comment which regularly appears as these cumulative folders are examined: "When he really wants to do something that he is interested in, he has no trouble learning." That sentence coupled with the words above it are now like a red flag to those of us who genuinely believe that there are dyslexic children and they as all other children want to learn, and find learning self-rewarding.

What did happen to the dyslexic children of yester-year? Different things happened. Some who were very bright learned enough compensations by themselves to get by very well.

Some became the "plodders," and what a negative effect it had, when a child heard that he was a plodder. The plodders went over and over any notes they could manage to take; they stayed a long time on every page, trying to get some sort of meaning; they copied their homework over and over. When describing these children, adults called them "slow but sure." They said that it took them a long time to learn anything, but once they learned it they could remember it for a long time.

Some of the dyslexics repeated every grade until they looked out of place because they were bigger than the other children. Then, they dropped out of school and the adults, including the truant officer, looked the other way.

Do you believe? Perhaps I can help you become a believer?

What Is Dyslexia?

It is my well-documented belief that there is a combination of characteristics which, taken together, make up a syndrome composed of poor academic achievement, left-right confusion, weak lateralization, and some degree of spatial disorientation. This is the condition which I call dyslexia. Most often, the immediate problem is an inability to read. This may also be accompanied by letter or number reversals, mirror writing, hyperactivity, or an emotional problem. I, along with others, have observed this in many children and also in adults, and I can make an objective analysis of this by a variety of standardized tests.[6]

I am aware that there are poor readers who do not have the other attributes which characterize dyslexia. I feel sure that there are also people who have poor spatial orientation, left-right confusion and weak lateralization who apparently had no trouble learning to read. This does not weaken my belief in the dyslexia syndrome.

It is my belief that dyslexia is not a dichotomy, but is a continuum, as are so many other human conditions. For example, there is no standardized test which is adequate for judging whether or not a person is hyperactive, because hyperactivity can vary in frequency and intensity in the same person, depending upon the environmental factors with which the hyperactive person is dealing. There is no black-and-white, yes-or-no way to judge hyperactivity except at the extremes. The same is true of dyslexia. Some people are mildly inconvenienced by their dyslexic tendencies, and others are almost incapacitated in their attempts to learn. I know, from first-hand experience, a number of cases in which a family has a grandfather, a father, and a son who are functionally illiterate, even though all are bright, alert people who function remarkably well in their lives. They get married and get jobs which support their families. They know they are handicapped, but they work out tremendously innovative ways of compensating for their handicaps. Therefore, I believe dyslexia is inherited, probably sex-linked, and may well be influenced by the relative development of dominance between the two hemispheres of the brain.

My observations of dyslexic people have led to a strong belief that human beings are capable of almost unlimited ways of compensating for their difficulties. A positive self-image is a basic requirement for the persistence necessary to make workable compensations, and these compensations are more effective when they are encouraged and aided at an early age.[4] It is possible to break out of the carapace of a poor self-concept, and people of all ages are capable of making some positive changes in their beliefs about themselves and of making a decision to learn to read. Probably no one ever had a completely positive self-image, and certainly all of us have handicaps of some kind. Hyperactivity often has a physical basis, but we know that it is possible for hyperactive people to learn ways of controlling and dealing with their hyperactivity. In a similar way, dyslexic people learn to "take charge" of their own learning processes, even when they cannot put into words what they do.

I knew one little girl who did all her reading sitting up in a tree. Nothing could swerve her from her course when she had something she wanted to read. Her parents were concerned about her when the weather was cold or when it was raining, but she was adamant. She had no way to tell her parents that she was so easily distracted that she simply could not concentrate while her father listened to the news, her mother rattled the dishes, her brothers argued, and her sister practiced her music. Dyslexic children seem to take in stimuli at such an acute level that the world must be screened out because they can absorb just one thing at a time. This little girl is grown now, but her emotional and sensory circuits still get overloaded. She has learned some adult equivalents of climbing a tree to get away from human stimuli.

I have another strong belief about the way dyslexic people learn.[1] Most people will agree that it is helpful to know the difference between left and right before trying to learn to read and write. People who work with children notice that it is difficult for children to learn to read when they cannot identify and copy simple geometric shapes. However, I have seen children who could "put the cart before the horse," so to speak. Learning to read helped them learn the movement of left to right, and helped them learn to differentiate shapes. For example, when getting acquainted with small children, I often administer the *Marianne Frostig Developmental Test of Visual Perception*, partly because it is so much fun for me and for the children. It is the only test booklet I have which children ask to take home with them. It gives me some useful information about a child and offers a vivid illustration to show to parents when explaining why the child is feeling frustrated. I am often given the opportunity to start right in and teach that child to read. After learning to read, the child is usually retested on the Frostig, and the change is dramatic. On the second-time-around, the child will often "Ace" the test, sailing right through it, without any errors. Such outstanding progress would not usually take place just because a child has lived for three or four months longer, unless something new had been added. So, it helps reading to have a good sense of directionality, but it also helps the sense of directionality to learn to read. Such is the beautifully flexible adaptability of the human mind.

Dyslexia is often spoken of as a handicap, but there is another side to this coin. Dyslexic people are more vulnerable, but they are also uncommonly sensitive to the feelings and needs of others. They are more aware of the colors, smells, and sounds about them. Perhaps that is why they may be unusually good teachers, good physicians, good spouses and good parents. They do over-react at times, but they are sometimes able to put this intensity of feeling into beautiful paintings, sculpturing or writing. We all know people who did not seem to shine at academic pursuits who, nevertheless, experienced unusually important accomplishments in fields of human relations. It has become a cliché to say that people should be accepted as individuals, but cliches are sometimes the outward signs of a deep universal belief. When treated as individuals, the prognosis for a dyslexic having a good life is excellent.

When we gradually come to realize that the word "dyslexia" is an emotional word to many people, would it not be better to use one of the euphemisms, such as "learning disability," "word blindness," "visual-perceptual-motor handicap," or "minimal brain dysfunction"? No, I think we should stick to the one word which cannot be misleading. Why? If I were the parent of a brain-damaged child I would certainly have every right to feel that my child's learning was disabled, and to feel that my child could correctly be classified as having a learning disability. If I then read that there were compensations for this condition which could alleviate it, I would feel that my child should have this training, and I would try to get it. In order to avoid confusion, it seems to me that we must separate these two entirely different handicaps.

If we use the expression "minimal brain dysfunction," we run the risk of being guilty of using words as a smoke screen to keep people from knowing what we mean. The main thought that many people have when they hear "minimal brain dysfunction" is that someone's brain is not functioning, and if the brain is not functioning, that person must be mentally retarded. *Dyslexia* and *Dyslexic* are somewhat difficult to pronounce, but so was *appendicitis* the first time we heard it. Words are supposed to be used to help people communicate, so let us say what we mean in the most precise, accurate way we can. Let us call it *dyslexia* (difficulty with words), and let us strive to use every helpful, kind, thoughtful, constructive way we can devise to communicate to the non-believers what we mean by the term.

Since most dyslexic people do not know they have a handicap, they are unable to understand themselves, and cannot help others understand why they often do things which seem strange. Sometimes they "lose" a word; not a new, long, complicated word which anyone might forget, but an ordinary, everyday sort of word. If your father were an engineer, and you had used the word hundreds of times, how would you explain not being able to call up the word "engineer" when asked your father's occupation?

Sometimes they scramble up the letters of a word, and stand there uncomprehending when everyone laughs. I know a Junior High School boy who announced the name of his oral report, and was shocked to hear the entire class, including the teacher, laugh. He walked out, vowing never to get up before a group again; and, if possible, never to go back to school. He explained to me, "I only said I was going to talk about *The Indian Torritery*. What's funny about that?"

Sometimes they hand in papers with the spelling so strangely jumbled that no one, not even a compassionate teacher, can figure out what the words are. Sometimes they can read aloud fairly well, but when asked to read silently they are unable to gain meaning from the words.

A dyslexic person *is* different from other people. It is not difficult for adults to understand that children with poor vision or poor hearing have special problems with learning, but it is often hard for them to believe that a bright, well-coordinated child who sees, hears, and comes from an advantaged home, could have great difficulty learning on a level close to his potential.

Many people connect dyslexia only with reading ability. If a child can read aloud rather well, adults often assume that this rules out a "learning disability." We must look further and observe more closely as the child goes through learning procedures. The difficulty may show up most strikingly in mathematics. Numbers and groups of numbers are symbols, just as letters and words are symbols for concepts and ideas.

Sometimes parents are told that their child "never finishes her work," or "won't try to copy problems off the board correctly," or "is not motivated to learn." These indictments are not given because the teacher does not want to help children learn; they are given when nothing that is tried seems to work. When a teacher has tried to make the work interesting, seemingly without success, rewards and punishments are tried. When none of these produce the desired results, there is a report to the parents that the child "doesn't want to learn." This makes the parents feel that they have, somehow, failed. Then we have the teacher, the parents, and the child feeling helpless and troubled.

It sometimes happens that, in this frustrating situation, the parents begin to blame the teacher and the teacher begins to blame the parents. All of them manage to convey to the child that most of the problem is his fault. Often children seem willing to take the blame; they may accept without question the accusation that they are lazy, unmotivated or not very intelligent. One boy of eleven explained to me: "My efforts are sporadic and inadequate." He had asked his friend to read to him what was written on the back of his report card, and had memorized it!

When a child really accepts the blame, she must also accept the reasons given by these adults she trusts, and this may become a self-fulfilling prophesy. Putting the blame in the "right" place is not helpful if there are no suggested ways to remedy the situation.

Too often the only ways suggested are to "try harder," Do you remember "trying harder" to stay up on roller skates? Trying harder does not help at all, but it is quite possible for a skilled teacher to show a novice the best way to place the feet, shift the weight, and pull with the correct muscles, so that almost anyone can skate adequately within a very few hours. The teacher shows ways to compensate for the fact that the feet are not firmly planted on the floor, and teaches a new way to move forward and backward without picking up the feet and placing each one ahead of the other as is done in walking.

In the same sort of way, dyslexic children can be taught compensations and new approaches to their problems, so that they can deal effectively with symbols such as numbers and letters.

If a child cannot seem to get meaning by reading small black squiggles on a white page, then we try to make it possible for that child to learn by reading aloud, by being read to, and by listening to tapes. For some, just having the print larger, with bigger spaces between the words and lines, makes it possible to get more meaning from the printed word.

It is important to think of dyslexia as a relative condition. Is there anyone who has not forgotten something or reversed something, or become confused, or been thoroughly lost? If these things happen to you rarely, then try calling up these times in order to make the plight of a dyslexic person less humorous. If you have ever read a sign, then passed it and realized that it could not possibly have said what you "read," you can begin to develop an understanding and a little tenderness for the person who has this happen frequently.

What Dyslexia Looks Like to the Parent

A parent is usually the first person to be aware that there is something wrong with the way a child is learning. What does the condition of dyslexia look like to an alert parent? We need to be careful when we list specific "symptoms," for no two children have exactly the same set of behaviors. There is really nothing strange about this. Each person is born with a unique genetic make-up, even in the case of identical twins. Each person has a unique self-image, because each of us has different experiences and different interactions with other people. Therefore, behavior patterns are also unique. With this in mind, there are some behaviors which cause parents to notice that things are not going as they should.

During preschool years, children are becoming social human beings. We watch with pleasure as they learn to get along well with other children, learn to share, learn to take turns and learn to verbalize their needs and feelings. Their learning is facilitated by having their questions answered, and we begin to notice that their questions become more and more complex. When there are minor difficulties parents usually work these out by discussions with family members.

Symptoms which may suggest to a parent that a preschool child may one day be classified as a dyslexic include such things as mixed laterality—that is, no positive preference for use of the right or left hand. Similarly, there may be mixed dominance—that is, the child may be right-handed and left-footed. Although the child does not know how to spell, words may be mispronounced—"valinna" for "vanilla," "bicsit" for "biscuit," or "torritery" for "territory." Another attribute may be an inability to follow a sequence of instructions. If the child is asked to place a marble in a bowl, bring a book to his mother, and then to close the window, he may skip the first two orders and follow only the third. In fact, if such sequencing is tried, it may be found that the child simply cannot follow more than a single instruction given at one time. These are among the things that a parent might look for prior to the time that a child enters school.

For a dyslexic child this picture usually begins to change with the beginning of school. Depending upon the severity of the handicap, there are often reports from the teacher that the child does not pay attention, cannot sit still, and disturbs other children. Parents usually react by having a good talk with the child, and explaining that it is important to try to learn well in school, and sometimes this seems to help a little for a short time.

During the first two years many parents are apt to adopt a "wait and see" attitude, unless the child begins to dislike school. Dawdling over getting ready for school, but bounding happily out of bed on Saturday may cause parents to begin to feel concerned. Shel Silverstein's[9] poem must have been written with a dyslexic child in mind:

SICK*

"I cannot go to school today,"
Said little Peggy Ann McKay.
"I have the measles and the mumps,
A gash, a rash, and purple bumps.
My mouth is wet, my throat is dry.
I'm going blind in my right eye.
My tonsils are as big as rocks,
I've counted sixteen chicken pox
And there's one more—that's seventeen,
And don't you think my face looks green?
My leg is cut, my eyes are blue—
It might be instamatic flu.
I cough and sneeze and gasp and choke,
I'm sure that my left leg is broke.
My hip hurts when I move my chin,
My belly button's caving in,
My back is wrenched, my ankle's sprained,

---

*"Sick," from *Where the Sidewalk Ends* by Shel Silverstein. Copyright© 1974 with permission from Harper and Row.

My 'pendix pains each time it rains.
My nose is cold, my toes are numb,
I have a sliver in my thumb.
My neck is stiff, my spine is weak,
I hardly whisper when I speak.
My tongue is filling up my mouth,
I think my hair is falling out.
My elbow's bent, my spine ain't straight,
My temperature is one-0-eight.
My brain is shrunk, I cannot hear.
There is a hole inside my ear.
I have a hangnail, and my heart is—what?
What's that? What's that you say?
You say today is . . . Saturday?
G'bye, I'm going out to play."

Yet even this classic picture does not always hold true. There are, of course, many kinds of children who do not want to go to school, and there are dyslexic children who never voice such a complaint.

Quite often, children who find that they are not learning as well as is expected become irritable or stubborn at home. Perfectly reasonable requests to help with household tasks may meet a short fuse, triggering an explosion. Reports from school begin to indicate that the child is not finishing the assigned work, will not try, is immature, and does not seem to be "motivated."

At this point, parents begin to wonder what has happened to the outgoing, exuberant child who was once so full of fun. As they discuss the behavior with their friends, they get a plethora of advice. One says, "I wouldn't put up with that from any child. If you let him get away with that now, think what may happen when he gets to be a teenager!"

This advice may send the formerly easy-going parent into a session of punishments, all designed to make the child see that this kind of behavior will not be tolerated. Parents scold, take away privileges, and spank. It may help for a short time, but then the behavior begins to get worse.

At this point, someone can be counted on to say, "Get off his back! Maybe he is a late bloomer. Let him grow up happy. He'll learn when he is ready." This seems logical, so Daddy tries to be a pal. There are fishing trips and picnics and peace at the dinner table. Again, this seems to work—for a short time.

Then, here comes another unsatisfactory report card with uncomplimentary remarks on the back. Now what? Obviously they must be doing something wrong; it seems to be rather easy to convince young parents that the whole thing reflects their incompetence as parents. Perhaps each of us has a lurking suspicion that we have done many things wrong as parents. Each one may blame the other for all the things which have or have not been done. One almost universal accusation is that the father does not spend enough time with the child. This is difficult to refute, for no one knows how much time a child needs. This guilt-producing complaint may be countered with the accusation that the mother does not give out enough discipline. All the pent-up frustrations of parenthood can boil over in a non-productive frenzy of anxiety. Even a young child can sense that she is the focus of all of these negative feelings, and anxiety deepens in her outlook.

Now the various family members begin to notice that there are other things about this small person which are different. She forgets things, things which everyone is sure she once knew. Someone has helped her learn her spelling words each week, but when there is a test which covers the work of several weeks, strange scrambled words are written. When she is told to go into another room to get something, she is found playing in the other room, having forgotten what she went for.

When she comes home from school, she is asked what she did at school that day, and she answers, "Nothing special." When pressed for details, she seems unable to recall any sort of sequence of the events of the day. Since she has no trouble remembering the time and day of any particular TV program, it is assumed that she has no interest in school. Someone may discover that she is eight years old and still does not know how to tell time. Sometimes she prints her letters and numbers backwards. Sometimes she pronounces words incorrectly, words which she has seen printed many times.

What is the matter with you? Why do you act this way? What are we going to do with you?

Myths About Learning
or
Things We Have Always Known About Learning that Are Not True

It seems fitting that this chapter should begin a discussion of myths about learning which serve to diminish the job of learning for all children. But a child who is dyslexic often lives with the basest of all human emotions—fear. In an unpredictable world, populated by unpredictable people, the dyslexic cannot trust even his own perceptions. His defeats keep him from developing love, compassion, and even hope. What are the facts about learning that we must grasp before fear develops into despair?

Let us put to rest some old myths about learning which have been around too long. Some of these are strangely persistent, with their origins buried deep in our Puritan ethic, which in turn goes back to the older concept that the world is a "vale of tears." Let us take these myths one at a time, and determine how real people act and learn.

Myth One: Learning is unpleasant.

What a lot of nonsense! Healthy, secure children have strong urges to learn. If they are allowed to find satisfaction in testing their abilities to explore, and are helped to channel their urges in safe, interesting ways, they grow into adults who find satisfaction in exploring and learning.

Learning is really fun. As each new skill is learned the door is opened to another one. Each time we successfully undertake a new enterprise, we become more self-confident that we can handle the next learning situation. With each broadening of our understanding, we learn to respect our own abilities more, and to strengthen our resolves to continue our growth. The happiest people in the world are those who are continually learning more about themselves and the world about them, so that they have no time to spend upon petty pursuits of revenge, maliciousness, or self-pity.

Myth Two: Learning is best accomplished by sitting in a chair listening to someone talk, or by sitting quietly reading.

Very little important learning takes place this way, but oh how hard it is to uproot this myth! Over and over research studies have shown that people learn best when they *experience* things, *use* things, *do* things, try out new ideas, discuss and "play around" with personal ways of applying new concepts. Pick out anything you can remember learning well and think about how it became meaningful to you. The odds are great that you did not sit listening to a speaker tell you what you should know, make some notes on a piece of paper about it, and then accept it, thereafter holding it as an important learning experience in your life.

Have you ever tried to talk about color to a person who has always been blind? Eventually, you will become convinced that no real understanding of color can be taught unless the other person can *experience* color. We cannot teach children how to become responsible citizens by merely talking to them. They must have opportunities to interact with other people, and to make decisions. No one can learn to drive a car merely by reading about it in a book. No one can gain real knowledge of history or math or literature until those subjects become part of their real-life experiences. A surprisingly large number of small children today can tell you the rights of a suspected criminal, largely because the world of crime and violence has become part of their personal experience through the television screen.

Myth Three: Failure toughens children and makes them strong. Life is full of failures and they should get used to it.

This myth is responsible for untold heartache, sorrow, and desperation among children. Perhaps it would help if we substituted another, more valid, aphorism: "There's nothing that succeeds like success." The opposite side of this coin is that there is nothing so apt to fail as a failure.

I like to think of failure and success as a kind of emotional bank account. Each time a child tries hard and fails there is a withdrawal from the plus side in the child's emotional bank account. Every time a child makes an honest effort and is successful, or even partially successful, there is a deposit in that account. Success is what makes us strong, not failure. If you can thoroughly convince a child that she is no good at something, it is then easier to convince that child that she is no good at other things. If you can make this over-all picture cover all the things which she thinks are important, you will not have a strong, persevering child; quite the contrary. You will have a loser, a quitter, a person who is licked before she starts.

If you are thinking about stories of famous men and women who overcame great odds to accomplish important things, delve further into the accounts of their lives. If you can find out enough, you will probably find that they did not think of themselves as failures; they saw themselves as able to overcome obstacles. Lincoln had to study by the light of a fire, but his studying brought him success, not failure. Clara Barton had to stand up to ridicule and disdain, but she had been strengthened by her parents to feel that her talent for healing was important and very special.

Myth Four: To really learn something, drill on it, over and over.

This does not work. Most of the time spent drilling is wasted. Actually, it is worse than wasted, for the child who is monotonously repeating something many times often builds up a hostility toward the material and will avoid any further contact with it.

Most of us have been the victims of this myth, and remember going over and over material which became more boring with every repetition. After a while the mind leaves the material, retaining only enough consciousness to keep the hand moving the pencil or the voice saying the words to be memorized. When this happens, mistakes creep in, and these mistakes are then memorized. Thus, the time may be used to memorize mistakes, which is worse than useless.

Does this mean that nothing should be memorized? Of course not, for knowing by memory such things as the multiplication tables saves us many hours of counting up answers to problems which should be done quickly and accurately. How does one memorize without tedious drill? The answer to that lies within each individual, for drill is helpful only so long as the individual is attending to the material at hand. As children become more self-confident from numerous successful sessions of learning, the attention span is apt to lengthen, and the student can concentrate for longer and longer periods with memory work. Just as soon as the attention wanders, the deleterious effects of drill begin.

Teachers can help by sharing all the ways which have worked for them as they have tried to increase their own powers of concentration. Students should be encouraged to share with each other the techniques they have worked out for memorizing. Here is a place for humor, if you can manage it. If you can think of a funny rhyme or memory aid, try it out, and the sillier the better.

If you had to learn when the Magna Carta was signed, did you have a special way to remember? I imagined a restaurant named the Magna Carta, and pictured a sign on the front door saying Magna Carta Lunch: 12:15. I had no trouble with the date of 1215 after that.

One little girl needed to learn where her mother worked and the phone number, in case she needed to call her. We used the tune of "Old McDonald" to sing:

My mother works for Williams and Mattox,
At the Surrency Building.
My mother works for Williams and Mattox,
At the Surrency Building.
With a 294-3278
With a 294-3278
My mother works for Williams and Mattox
At the Surrency Building.

That ended the problem of losing the slip of paper with the information on it.

Ideally, all learning would come about because the material to be learned was intrinsically interesting, or was such that the student could see immediate need for the knowledge. No one who has ever tried to teach can be so naive. We all know there are basic facts which must be memorized if children are to be able to move freely and effectively in the world. No one ever mastered a musical instrument, learned the multiplication tables or became a good athlete without practice. But practice and memorization are not the same as mindless drill.

When a tennis player works to perfect a backhand stroke, little will be accomplished if the player is mentally engrossed in an unfinished mystery novel. The golfer who tries to address the ball with a smooth stroke will not improve if other matters crowd out the attention which should be focused upon the bodily stance, the grip on the club and the eye on the ball. The tedious piano drills which were once responsible for so many children dropping out of participating in music have now been replaced by techniques for interspersing the skills which must be repeated with the playing of tunes which will produce pleasing results quickly.

As the piano student becomes more and more successful, there is engendered a desire for more challenging work. This is accompanied by a sense of pride in learning to increase the concentration necessary to stay for longer intervals when practicing exercises for improving motor skills and reading increasingly difficult music. As the musician becomes more skilled, there is an increase in the approval and acclaim of other people, which is added to the self-satisfaction in a job well done. As a result, we now have groups of very young children happily learning to play violins together, and we are seeing a resurgence of interest in music for people of all ages. The very first music lesson can be enjoyable, and each lesson thereafter can have some moments of success and pleasure. The more fun it is, the harder the student will work.

Self-Concept and Learning

If the brain were really like a computer, with our sensory organs feeding it raw data consisting of touch, sounds, sights, and smells, then the "print-out" would always be the same. If five people were together in a room, and something happened which could be picked up by one or more of the five senses, each person would experience about the same thing. Therefore, each would describe it in approximately the same way, but we know that this does not happen. If there are five people involved in a car accident, there will be five different stories of what happened, and each will wonder why the others did not perceive it as it "really" happened.

We may look at one of the cars and see that there is a damaged part on the left front fender. However, it is quite possible that one person would perceive this "fact" as minor damage, and another as extensive damage. One person might feel very emotional about it and another might feel it only as a minor irritation in a day filled with much more important things. The speed of the car would be a hard fact, but the perception of the speed might well vary from "much too fast," through "moderate," to "rather slow." Some may see this disparity as human error, faulty perception, or inattention, and insist that reality will be found if we only look diligently. Although there are some things which are factual reality, and would be recognizable as facts by almost everyone, such facts make up only a very small part of our perceptions.

For example, we might look at a chair. How can a chair be perceived in different ways? Surely, it is a piece of raw data, the same today as it will be tomorrow. But, from the point of view of a person entering the room and wanting to sit down, it may be seen merely as a place to sit. If, however, it is seen by an artist it may be seen as a total design, composed of lines, color and form, pleasingly arranged or not. An engineer might see it in regard to its stresses and strains, and consider the amount of weight it will safely hold. To one who manufacturers chairs it might be seen as a commodity which would require a certain amount to manufacture and could be sold for a certain amount of profit.

What determines the way in which we perceive objects and events? We each "see" things according to our past experiences and according to our concepts of ourselves and others. We act in the way we do because of our perceptions at the moment of our behavior.

Translated another way, this means that everybody, including children, is always doing his best, according to the way in which he perceives the situation. Once this concept of doing one's best is accepted, it becomes evident that much of the blame we attach to people is unproductive, for no one can behave in any way except the way which is determined by his perceptions of the past and his perceptions of the moment.

This is a tremendously important concept, and one which is often overlooked when people are trying to determine the cause for something which happened.

If we can accept the idea that everyone is always doing his best, why is it that we do not all think the same behavior is right or wrong? We all perceive the world in the way we do primarily because of our self-concepts.

If I could ask you what kind of person you are, you might tell me that you are an ordinary, average person, but the chances are that you do not really feel that this is true. You probably know that you are special and unique. If I press you for further characteristics, you might tell me what your job is, where you went to school, whether you are married or not, and whether or not you have children. You might tell me that you enjoyed watching the World Series, that you like your potatoes hash-browned and your eggs sunny-side-up. These are probably all surface things, some of which can be easily changed. They are part of your self-concept, but are probably not the deep, inner part which makes you different from all other people.

What is a self-concept, and how is it formed? Self-concept is how you see yourself, and it is formed primarily by interaction with other people; it begins as soon as an individual begins reacting to another person, which is at birth. You have heard people say, "I'm no good at math." You may have thought, "I wish more people liked me." Or even, "I never do anything right."

If you have had these feelings, they are among the negative parts of your self-concept. You may want to protest and say, "What if they are true?" They are true only if they become a self-fulfilling prophesy. If you are unable to learn to swim it is because you see yourself as a non-swimmer; if you are disliked it is because you see yourself as a person who is not likable.

Sometimes we can think back to our early years and remember exactly when and why we began to think of ourselves as unworthy and incapable in some areas. Unfortunately, our teachers are often among the ones we remember as being those who started our feelings of inadequacy.

How far back must we go to find the beginnings of the self-concept? Long before a baby can talk we can tell that the baby knows and responds to the mother's voice and the sound of the baby's name. Even before that, babies seem to need to know that they are loved, and they seem to learn that they are loved by whether or not they are touched and talked to. They do not think, in words, "I must be lovable because someone is cuddling me and talking to me." The words are not there, but the feelings are, for babies may die when only their physical wants are taken care of.

Every day we live, and each time we interact with others, our self-concepts are affected. How much they are affected depends upon how important that other person is in our perceptual field.

Every time we succeed at something which is important to us, we make a deposit in our emotional bank account. Each time we are diminished by something someone does or says we make a withdrawal. Some people, some children, are always in the red, always overdrawn. The young man in the news who chopped up eight nurses was a damaged human being. He knew that he was was rotten, detestable, and vicious. He became that way because he thought he was that way. In order that he might never forget it, he had tattooed on his arm, "Born to Lose." This was a self-fulfilling prophesy; he knew he was that way and he had to be sure that everyone else knew it too. He showed all of us what he was really like, and we were convinced. He was a loser. He lost.

On occasion, each of us has, no doubt, wondered why someone else has acted in a particular way. You may have watched a child behaving in a manner which seems to bring nothing but trouble to everyone, including the child. You may have wondered why that child would behave in a way which seems to be self-destructive. Yet, most of us have had the experience of looking back upon something we ourselves have done, and have asked ourselves, "Why did I do that?"

What does all this have to do with helping dyslexic children, or with teaching anyone? The self-concepts of children are affected every day by the important adults with whom they interact. During school years the self-concept is still quite flexible, and the child is very vulnerable. I happen to believe that we are all more vulnerable than we seem, but as adults we have practiced hiding our vulnerability. Every adult who works with children is a potential changer of self-concepts. Think back to your early years. You may not remember what your teachers looked like, but I wager that you know how each teacher felt about you.

Dyslexics are among the most vulnerable people in our society. There are several reasons for this. There are certain actions and specific types of learning which are now expected of all children. Among the most important of these is the ability to communicate by means of written and spoken language, and the ability to handle numbers well enough to meet the needs of a complex society. This has not always been true.

During the early years of our country's beginning, "book learning" was often seen as an unimportant luxury, or even as something to be avoided. We have gradually widened our vision of reading to the point that we feel a strong effort should be made to teach all children to read, and to read as well as they can. We see reading as a method of acquiring a type of freedom; the person who can read has many more alternatives in life than the one who cannot. There is knowledge and satisfaction which are available only to those who can read. Parents are often willing to go without all sorts of important things in order to assure their children of a good education, and when we say "education" we automatically include reading.

During the first week in September, all over the United States, there are thousands of children who walk into school buildings for the first time, confident that the skill of reading will be explained and transmitted so that all the wonderful things in books will become available. And this is what happens for most children, at varying rates of speed. But for dyslexic children, the beginning of school may be the beginning of a process of confusion and anxiety. Picture to yourself a six-year-old who has been told that he will learn to read in first grade, and who watches the other children doing just that. For him, it does not seem to be working. He is hearing the same words that the other children are hearing; he is seeing the same things that others are seeing. But they seem to be doing something which he cannot do, and he does not know why. What would you do in such a situation? Try harder? Bluff a little? Try to turn the attention to something you could understand? Avoid going back the next day? Pretend that you did not care? The children do all of these, but one by one their defenses and their excuses are shot down by the adults, stripping away all the protective coverings and leaving only a child who is not learning. These children learn early to live with shame and guilt. When we feel ashamed and guilty we begin to dislike ourselves. When we dislike ourselves we also dislike others. As adults, if we are unable to perform well at our jobs, and therefore dislike our jobs, we usually have an option of quitting. We do not allow children this option, and school is the only job in town for children. Few adults would go on, day after day, trying over and over to do something which is as difficult as reading is for the dyslexic child. It is a constant source of wonder to me that children keep giving us another chance after days, weeks, months and years of frustrating attempts to master a skill which is so elusive.

Children become more and more vulnerable as their best efforts lead only to confusion and embarrassment. They believe that we have the right to expect them to learn to read, and they feel inadequate when, despite so much effort from adults, they fall short of the mark. Often there are attempts on the part of the child to mollify the adults by trying to make up for their deficiencies by putting forth great effort to show everyone that there are other things which they can do. ("Look at me. Watch me turn somersaults.

Want to hear me sing? Look, I'm straightening up the books on the shelf. Look at my muscles.")

Sooner or later it is made clear to the child that none of his tricks make up for not reading, and then it is a short step toward feeling that he is not a worthy, capable or "good" person. Incompetence breeds incompetence, and a negative self-concept brings the attitude that there is no point in trying.

Learning About the Brain

When we think about learning most of us think of the brain as the organ which does the learning, the thinking and the organizing. And so it is, but is it not astonishing that your brain would try to understand itself? Your big toe and your ear do not try to understand themselves. We can look at a lung and realize that it is shaped in a way which makes it possible to hold and expel air, and my knee looks like something which can allow my leg to bend, but a brain does not look very useful. It looks a little like a shelled walnut, stuck up there on top of the brain stem. It is damp and convoluted, a pinkish grey in color with the folds connected by neural tissues. It weighs about three pounds and contains billions of nerve cells, which can communicate with other nerve cells. This tiny "telephone switchboard" manages to organize all our fears, hopes, desires, ideas, dreams and actions. Right now, my brain is making it possible for me to write these words about itself and then your brain makes it possible for you to read about itself.

The brain is often compared to a computer, with the analogy that our sensory organs send in raw data of sounds, smells, tastes and sights so that the brain can organize and interpret it. The brain cannot respond to all stimuli, for hundreds of messages may be sent in at once. The brain stem monitors the stimuli so that the brain can interpret the meaningful data. Who receives the print-out from the data? The brain does! It also stores in its memory bank the items it considers important, and decides what action should be taken concerning the information it has received.

Continuing the analogy of the brain as a computer, consider what might happen if the brain-computer received as data the letter "b." Instead of decoding it as a vertical line with a half-circle on the right at the bottom, what if it sends out the print-out with the information that the half-circle is on the left at the bottom? That makes it a "d" instead of a "b," and this can change the word, the sentence, and the concept symbolized by the sentence. Or, suppose the brain-computer decodes it as a line with a half-circle on the right at the top? This makes it a "p," which again confuses the concept.

Is it so strange that this wonderful computer does not always give a consistent print-out? To me, it seems marvelous that the print-outs are as regular as they are, as much of the time as they are. A person who is "color blind" (a term which can cover a great many deviations) does not see colors in the same way that most other people do. Rather than observing this as strange, it seems miraculous to me that so many of us seem to see colors in ways that appear to be very similar, although no one has been able to prove that this is so. I know one child who says that each color "matches" a note on the piano. I know a color-blind boy who consistently works the *Farnsworth Dichotomous Test for Color Blindness* in exactly the same order. He asked me if it could be possible that he was "correct" and all the other people were "wrong," a question I had trouble dealing with.

Perhaps this inconsistency of the print-out from the brain is the key to many of the difficulties which plague the dyslexic. If a "b" always looked like a "d" the brain would compensate for this quickly, as it does when we put on blue or pink-tinted glasses. We do not keep worrying about why everyone has a blue face or why all the formerly white houses now look pink; colors are adjusted for, by the brain-computer, and the world looks about the same as we remember it, which I think is a perfectly splendid feat for the brain to accomplish. But if a brain only occasionally decodes the word *boy* as *ydo*, all the phonics training in the world will not help the brain read the print-out it has sent itself. If a person perceives the number 257 on a chalkboard and copies it as 572, it is not helpful to tell the person who owns that particular brain that she is lazy or unmotivated.

In reality, we do not, of course, have a switchboard operator or a whirring computer encased in our skulls, and the analogy can be carried only so far. The brain of a six-year-old child is millions of times more complicated than the most elaborate computer ever devised, having more connections and interconnections than any machine. We ask

40

that child to look at a black letter on a white page, and to connect it with other letters. We expect him to connect all these to sounds, and also to ideas. We expect this to happen almost instantly, even though there are no letters which always have the same sounds, and there are no words which convey the same ideas to all people. There is not even any sort of universal language, and there is no spoken language which is stable or unchanging.

As we get older, and have set up millions of complicated connections in our brains, we become annoyed if we cannot instantly retrieve all facts, ideas, and thoughts which we once "knew." All those daily and nightly perceptions we expect to be stored, labeled and interrelated with all other perceptions, and then we expect them to be coming right down the conveyor belt when we want them!

When did people begin to think about their brains? Or when did people begin to use their brains so think about their brains? Lacking a "logical" answer to that question, it is likely that this began to take place soon after language developed, for then, very soon, people had to think about what their language would mean to another person, and to try to interpret the language to other people. It is very much a part of our speech today. We speak of "brainy" people, and teachers tell children to "use their brains."

For a long time we have been taught that the left hemisphere governs the right side of the body and the right hemisphere takes care of the left side. As the brains of the researchers have delved more deeply into this subject, however, the findings have become more complex. Most people are right-handed, and for most people the left hemisphere is used for verbal and analytic thought. The left hemisphere has more definite pathways which are more clearly defined than the right hemisphere. It is the left hemisphere that learns to read, to write and to talk. It also learns to use numbers and to think in ways which are logical and abstract. The left hemisphere has a slight elongation at the temple, which can be thought of as a "language lump." Would the brain of a Robinson Crusoe have as large a language lump as that of a television news broadcaster? In other words, do we start out with a very slight elongation which gets larger as it is used? We can only speculate.

The right hemisphere deals with visual and spatial abilities; it is involved in perceptions of art, music, sculpturing, and dancing. It also is responsible for hunches, gut reactions, and the ability to "see" an entity when only disparate parts are actually present. The nerve arrangement of the right hemisphere is more diffuse and less exact, but not less important, for it is there that creative, innovative ideas are originated.

It seems that actually we have two brains, but this is an oversimplification. A great many things that we do require the services of both cerebral hemispheres. Reading, for example, is in one sense a linear, logical language process, but it can also be a synthesizer of perceptual images, an invoker of images of beauty or ugliness, and a basis for an intuitive understanding of a new concept.

For nearly all people who are right-handed, right-footed and right-eyed, the differentiation between the left and right hemispheres is rather strong. But what about the one person in ten who is left-handed? Are the lefties mirror images of the righties? The answer is, "Sometimes." Jerre Levy[8] found that the lefties who write with the hand hooked, with the point of the pencil pointing toward the body, have language in the left side of the brain, and those who write with the eraser pointing over the shoulder have language in the right hemisphere. The occasional righty who uses an inverted posture has language in the right hemisphere.

To add to the complexity of the situation, there seem to be people who "prefer" one hemisphere over the other. If we are thinking in terms of "two brains," this might mean that one of the two is usually dominant over the other. Gur[7] found that when people break eye contact, they habitually move their eyes in one particular direction, according to which side of the brain is dominant. The eyes move to the left, if the right side of the brain is dominant; the right-movers have the left hemisphere dominant.

There have been no definitive studies concerning how the brains of dyslexic people differ from those of other people in regard to the functioning of the two sides of the brain. From my experience with dyslexics, I can hazard a guess that the two hemispheres may be less definitely lateralized for them than for other people. We can watch the way they attack learning problems and know for certain that they go about it in ways that differ from the ways other people work. Dyslexics, more than other people, seem to "lose" words; they "forget" the names of people they know well, and sometimes have to "hunt" for some common, every day words which they use often. We can speculate that when a person "draws a blank" when trying to remember something, it may be that neither one of the hemispheres is "minding the store." We may also speculate that stuttering or stammering might occur when both hemispheres are trying to function at once. The confusion and shame which suffuses the face of a dyslexic person, when sounds or ideas are scrambled, are familiar to all of us who work with them. Their confusion between left and right, and their inability to accurately place events in time frames must certainly have something to do with incomplete hemispheric laterality and dominance.

Since there is some sort of differentiation between the activities of the two hemispheres, and since it seems that people differ in how strongly lateralized their brains are, it would seem that there would be ample opportunities for the two sides to confict or to cooperate in dealing with a problem utilizing several kinds of thinking (as most problems do). There is much to be done before we can pin-point differences in individual brains, and even when some of the mysteries are cleared up there will still remain the neverending search for ways to help people use this knowledge for bettering the lives of children so that they can become more fulfilled, joyful human beings.

Reading and Writing are Important

There are many adults and children in our society who are unable to read or write, and there are many more who can do so only on a very low level. These people are always at a disadvantage. Now, more than ever before, people need to be able to understand what others have written, and to be able to record their own ideas and thoughts. Reading and speaking and writing cannot be separated. When we write something we must be able to read it. When we work with numbers we need to write them and read them.

Daniel Boone needed only a small written and spoken vocabulary, for most of his energies were expended in staying alive by acquiring food, providing himself with shelter, and making sure that wild animals did not attack him. Much of the necessary knowledge for these pursuits probably existed on a level which did not require speech, as he did not need to teach others or to record how he felt about what he was doing.

There are very few people today who live such a simple, uncomplicated life, and as life becomes more complicated the need for reading and writing increases. Our lives are intricately interwoven with those of other people, and those who cannot communicate by means of written and spoken words are cut off from many of the satisfactions of living.

Dyslexic children *can* be taught to read and write, and the dyslexic children who have grown into adulthood without reading can also be taught.[3] Techniques have to be a little more flexible, and teachers need to be more alert and sensitive, but these people have a right to learn, and those of us who come into contact with them have an obligation to help each one work out personal ways to succeed.

There is always some controversy about the best ways to teach reading, and this becomes more heated when the discussion centers around children who do not learn to read easily. The controversy is a healthy one when it sharpens an educator's efforts to find good ways to help children learn. But if there were one surefire technique for teaching dyslexics, it would have spread like wildfire, and every school would have complete instructions, as well as all required materials. Good teachers use many different ways to teach reading, writing, and numbers. It is a real advantage to anyone to be able to sound out words phonetically, for most people never cease to meet new words. However, when letters appear to scramble up into new combinations, phonics is not very helpful. It is also an advantage to be able to know a large number of words by sight, but if the processing of the letters on a page is erratic, these words may have several sight formations. It is an advantage to be able to scan material rapidly at times, but if increased speed does not result in comprehension and retention of what is scanned, scanning is an exercise in futility.

Teaching children to read should have a high priority, so our persistence in trying new ways should be infinite. If you are talking to a foreigner who knows little English, and want to help that person understand how to do something, the chances are that you will try a wide variety of ways to communicate, with the effort expended depending upon the importance of what you are trying to convey. When we talk to a foreigner, we sometimes find ourselves shouting, so we can be forgiven if we sometimes treat dyslexic children as if they were deaf. Just as we would apologize to the person whose native tongue is not English, we can clear the air with an apology when we catch ourselves raising our voices to children. A little humor helps, provided the children do not feel that the humor is diminishing to them.

Sometimes it helps to keep our real objectives clearly defined. However we teach, and whatever tools we use, the purpose is to help the child learn to read and write. The only way this can be accomplished is to provide opportunities for children to use language. If the teacher is the only one using the language, then the teacher's language skills are probably improving. If children do not have opportunities to form their own ideas into words, spoken and written and read, then their skills are probably not improving very much. Many people do not really know what they think or believe or feel until they hear themselves saying it. There are many adults who cannot express feelings and emotions because they did not have opportunities to practice this skill when they were children.

There was a time when the writing of letters was considered an important part of every educated person's life. We have been enriched by reading the compilations of letters written by great people. We gain insight into the Revolutionary War period when we read the letters of Abigail Adams to her husband. Winston Churchill becomes a vividly real person when we are able to read the letters which were saved by all the people with whom he found time to correspond. We shall all be the poorer if people stop writing love letters altogether, and stop putting on paper deeply felt emotions and convictions. Perhaps we will not need so many therapy sessions if children can be encouraged to begin early in life to sort out and express feelings and personal thoughts.

When children go on a field trip there is not *one* story to tell and to write and to read. Each child saw and felt and reacted differently. Making it possible for each child to verbalize and write in a personal way can be a personal goal for each of us when we try to help children use language. Some of the best ways I have been able to do this will be explained, to the best of my ability to communicate such a personal process, in the next chapters.

Junior and the Need to Learn

Healthy, secure people have strong urges to explore and to learn. They find it pleasurable to indulge these urges. This is true of other animals also. Many of you have lived with a pet which delighted you with its unending attempts to explore. I once shared a house with a hamster named Junior. Junior had a large cage with an exercise wheel, and it was well used. Junior had a well-balanced diet, and was regularly taken out to be patted and handled. What more could a hamster need?

From the first day it was obvious that this was not enough. Time after time, Junior got out of his cage, despite our best efforts to fasten it securely. When this happened, no place in the house was safe from his chewing and tearing. He had highly intellectual tastes in magazines, and liked my stack of Journals of the American Psychological Association. He gnawed at them until he had enough material to make a cozy nest in the tiny space behind the journals.

This was not an urge to hide from people, for he was often easy to catch after a night of exploring. When he was allowed to run free we watched admiringly while he worked for an indefinite period trying to get up the three steps which separated one part of the house from the other. Time after time, Junior would get his little paws over the edge of the slippery terrazo steps, only to fall on his back and start over. Eventually he made it, and was off for more adventures. Hamsters are handicapped by being able to see only about twelve inches, but this did not deter Junior from investigating every ledge and trail.

If we can accept a hamster's need to learn, surely the next step is the acceptance of the natural desire of children to explore and to learn. We do not need to motivate children to learn; like Junior, they are already motivated. As soon as each baby is physically able to learn a skill, there are

Junior with two of his admirers.

attempts to use the skill and then to perfect it. Learning is enjoyable, even at this early age.

If you have trouble accepting this, take time to observe an infant. Unless hampered, a healthy baby struggles constantly to change positions, to reach, to grab, to pull, and to find out as much as possible about the things or people which are near, including the taste. As soon as a a skill is developed and practiced, it is used to help in the development of other skills. Infants often keep this learning process going until they are exhausted. They sleep, and awaken to begin again, endlessly trying to learn.

When we lost Junior we always began looking for him in one of the places we had last found him. He was never there. Not once was that little animal satisfied to stay with the familiar, even though there were signs that he visited his old places before going on to find a new one. If a hamster needs variety, think how much more urgent it is for such a complicated animal as a child. Try this: Get two new toys for a baby. Use simple ones which do not have multiple uses. Give the baby one of them and let him handle it, suck on it, smell it and use it in all the ways babies have to get acquainted with a toy. Now remove the toy for a few seconds, and this time put both toys in front of the baby separated by about eighteen inches. Watch which one he reaches for. He will reach for the new toy, if I know babies, for surprise and new experiences are important even at infancy.

The activities of a baby learning to grasp a rattle may seem quite different from the attempts of a child to learn to read, but it is all part of the same process of exploring the environment. The baby develops into a preschool child who climbs, rolls, pulls things apart, tries to put things together, moves things, pushes, babbles, laughs and explores. There are, of course, some unpleasant times, when a child learns that some things are hot, and that falling hurts, but if adults take the time to set up a relatively safe, interesting play space, the joy of learning surpasses any small troubles.

Many parents watch this kind of learning with interest and pleasure, only to become grim when the child reaches the stage at which he is expected to learn the "important things" which are taught at school. Have you heard adults say things of this nature: "Children should understand that not everything can be fun. Some things are hard, and the sooner they find that out, the better." This is very much like maintaining that because one's own childhood was unpleasant, we should try to make childhood unpleasant for everyone.

If learning is a process which is satisfying, why is it that children, and especially dyslexic children, seem to resist learning things which we as adults can see are important? Hard things are boring. Why is learning sometimes hard? If there is not enough background knowledge, if steps have been skipped which cannot be bridged by the learner, then that kind of learning is hard, perhaps impossible. The obvious remediation for this is to supply the needed background just as soon as the gaps are discovered. We cannot learn calculus until we have learned arithmetic. Dyslexic children have more gaps than other children. When they do not accurately process the information on a page or on the chalkboard, they have a gap and are often unable to go ahead to the next level. Sometimes they cannot take notes or write down what is being said to them. They may get the first part of a sentence, but when they try to write it they find they cannot write and listen at the same time.

If learning is not seen as being relevant or important or interesting to the learner, then that learning will be hard, and it will also be forgotten quickly. When we have chosen some information or skill which we think is important for a child to learn, we must help that child see why this kind of information is exciting or worthwhile. If we are bored by it, but feel that we ought to teach it, the learner is not apt to be enthusiastic about it.

I am shocked when I hear a child say, "I hate English!" How can anyone hate the English language, which is such a marvelous way to communicate with other people? When we talk about it, I find out what the child really hates is "learning" about gerunds or participles or infinitives or prepositional phrases. For the dyslexic child, time is all too short to spend long hours on such a topic. All the energy spent in getting children to memorize definitions of parts of speech is often met by an even more energetic forgetting process.

The time to bring in the names of parts of speech is while we are using language for expressing ideas, understanding the ideas that other people have expressed, and recording important ideas and feelings. If you are learning to paint, you will learn the names of the colors and brushes, and if you are learning to repair a motorcycle you will use the names of the tools and the parts of the engine, right there on the spot. This will not be handled as a separate course of study. It would be frustrating indeed to work on a motor with someone and have to talk about "that long thing over there" or "that round, flat thing." If you could not find out a name for the parts, you would eventually make one up.

When children are personally involved in learning, problems and solutions come up in a natural way. Integrating all kinds of learning with the real stuff of living is especially important to a child who is handicapped by an inability to handle words, written or read, in a smooth, uninterrupted flow. It is doubly important for the results to be personally satisfying when the process of achieving is hampered by a difficulty in coordinating spoken and written words.

Children become involved in the learning process in individual ways, depending upon their past learning and upon their abilities as they see them. When you see them intent upon what they are doing, when you see them busy, when you hear them chuckling, you will know that they are having as much fun as Junior when he got his cage opened.

PART TWO

Teaching Dyslexic Children

I hear and I forget;

I see and I remember;

I do and I understand.

How Do You Teach
A Dyslexic to Read?

If I answer, it depends upon the child's age or what he likes to do or what he thinks he cannot do or wishes he could do, the questioner thinks I am evading the question. Often, I say, "Why don't you watch me?" I then fill the room with curious adults and sit down in the middle of the room with the child and *something interesting to do.* What I bring will be something I find interesting and something I think the child will find challenging and fun to investigate.

I spent an hour with a little girl one day, with an audience composed of all the teachers in an elementary school. We did all kinds of things, including cooking and beginning to play a flutaphone. At the end of the hour it seemed to me that there had been a great deal done in regard to reading and writing and numbers, but when I explained that this would be the way I would begin to teach this little girl to read, I did not feel that I had any good vibes from the teachers. I asked for some reactions. One said, "Who would clean up the mess?" I answered that I probably would, with some help from the little girl, if she had time. There were other questions, and I felt inadequate to interact with all those nice people that I liked so much. Finally, one young teacher said, "I think this was what they describe as a language arts experience." I felt deflated, for I had been having such a fine time, and I thought I was sharing such an enormously productive learning experience, and I could tell that they had all been waiting for the fun to be over and the lesson to start.

If these educated, open-minded teachers could not understand what I was doing or why I was doing it, then there had to be something wrong with my ability to communicate. There was. I did not know myself how to put into words how I know what to do when a dyslexic child cannot read. I needed to learn more in order to share my insights in a more effective way. Perhaps I could find out more about how I, myself, learn difficult new concepts. I certainly do not learn them by taking notes while someone lectures or simply by reading in a book, although that may help.

A great deal of research has been spent in trying to find out what kinds of things are done in the right and left hemispheres of the human brain. Apparently, for "normal" right-handed, right-footed, right-eyed people, the left hemisphere takes care of speech (written, spoken or thought about), mathematical processes, and step-by-step analytical thinking. The right hemisphere is good at artistic and musical development, gestalt synthesis, pattern recognition and holistic generalization. Of course, some processes need both kinds of thinking. For example, reading the notes of music is very similar to reading words, and probably both hemispheres work for a musician. Perhaps they sometimes alternate, or perhaps they sometimes work together.

Of course, if this is true of musicians, it must also be true of the really creative mathematicians! Mathematical geniuses do not spend their days working out math problems that other mathematicians have written down in workbooks. They do not spend so much time looking at the trees that they fail to see the forest; they can see the trees as entities, but they can visualize the entire forest, even all the forests on the earth, as one all-encompassing entity.

Now, at last I feel that I am getting close to understanding why I am successful at teaching the way I do. What if dyslexic people need to integrate the functioning of both hemispheres in order to cope with a new concept or a new pattern of learning? What if they need to *start* with right hemisphere processes in order to get the feel of the problem and then, after they have involved themselves deeply in actually *doing*, and experiencing, they can then shift over to the left hemisphere in order to verbalize or write or read what they have experienced?

I have no way to prove what I feel I know about these mental processes. Perhaps it is something altogether different. Perhaps dyslexic people are weakly lateralized, and are not inclined to separate problems into neat categories and assign them to one hemisphere or the other. Perhaps they are more apt than other people to involve the right hemisphere along with the left. I do not know exactly what happens, but I have a strong feeling that the organization of the two hemispheres *is* different for a dyslexic person. I know very well that this unusual organization of the hemispheres can sometimes create delightfully innovative ways of working and of looking at the world. This happens when the dyslexic is freed of the burden of being a non-reader in a world which too often equates reading skill with intelligence.

So—*how do you teach dyslexic children to read?* You (and I) get them totally, actively immersed in right hemispheric activities. They must feel it (eagerly), smell it, taste it, touch it, do something with it that makes something interesting happen. That "something interesting" can be something beautiful, something unexpected and surprising, something funny, something sensuous, or something exciting. Or it can be all of these. It cannot be something *watched.* The *learner* must be the one who mixes something, or discovers something or puts something together to make something new. This cannot be something done in an apathetic way. It must cause the learner to feel that he is making something happen. After this important experience the feelings can then be shifted over to the opposite hemisphere to verbalize, orally or on paper what has happened. Michelangelo and Leonardo Da Vinci, both dyslexic, *did* things. They sculpted and painted and constructed things. After they had immersed themselves in the exciting experiences, they verbalized them, but the words they wrote were pale things beside the activities which produced things which have caused people by the millions to stand rapt and ennobled by the chance to share the beauty that has stood the test of time.

What I Have Seen Others Do

For the past 10 years I have taken advantage of every chance I have had to observe outstanding teachers of dyslexic children. When I hear of an outstanding teacher I simply call and ask if I can come to visit, promising to either sit quietly or to help in any way I can, if I can only be allowed to watch. It's always fun to watch a skilled person, but I have been looking for something in particular. I have been trying to see if I can find something that all these good teachers have in common.

Some have told me that their success is due to an ability to incorporate music into the school day. Others have told me that art, and the use of many kinds of art materials is the secret of their success. One young man from the University of Florida told me that drama and mime are indispensible when working with learning-disabled children. In Miami I watched a magnificent teacher teaching 18 severely dyslexic children all day, five days a week. One of her legs is permanently stiff, and she wears heavy corrective shoes up almost to her knees. She also wears the most loving look on her face that I have ever seen on a human being.

I had been told that her class was made up of cast-off children that no one else could teach or manage. They ranged in age from 6 to 10. Her teaching was completely individualized. As the children came into the room in the morning they took off their shoes at the door and went to find her. She had no desk, so they looked around to find her. Together, they pulled out a big envelope from a file, with the child locating her name. The two of them talked quietly for a minute or two about what was in the envelope, for it contained the work of the day. There were about half as many chairs in the room as there were children. At the beginning of the year she had expected a class of 9, but it had slowly grown, and she said 18 chairs would unnecessarily clutter up the floor space. She said that no mother would line up her family in chairs, so why should she? One boy of nine put a bedspread over an easel and anchored it firmly with bricks, to make a sort of tent, into which he crawled with his envelope and his work. Other children sat or lay on the floor. Not once did I see all the chairs full. This teacher said she was successful because she was physically handicapped, and therefore understood what it was like to be different. She said the children felt very sorry that she could not remove her shoes as they could.

These fine teachers did not themselves know what they had in common. They were all so different, but they all have some traits in common. First, and most important, they all see themselves and all the children as interesting, worthwhile, capable, trustworthy people who are eager to learn. Each one of them saw each child in a positive way.

The second trait was one which almost escaped my notice, but when I did see it I could see that it makes all the difference in the world. Not a one of these teachers *ever* came to school empty-handed! What did they bring? They brought things that they themselves considered interesting. Somehow they imparted this interest to the children. I don't think any of them ever opened a package or tried out a new appliance except at school, and I hope you won't after you read this.

This was not an isolated "show and tell" time done to relieve the boredom of the regular curriculum; this *was* the curriculum. This kind of activity is contagious; I found myself looking for things that I could contribute to the classes. We all need to be appreciated, and I can promise you that you will be enthusiastically greeted and appreciated if you become known as a person who brings a piece of your outside world into the school each day.

What will you do with it? Resist the temptation to lecture about it. Use it. When a child asks what it is for, say, "Watch!" and go on using it. Let someone help you and gradually withdraw and let it be passed around.

For these children, the brain is not neatly divided into two areas which can separate and deal with stimuli. Mixed dominance is characteristic of dyslexia. For a person with mixed dominance, learning is not accomplished effectively by merely listening, reading and writing. There is a greater need to bring in other skills, activities involving body movement, touch, taste, smell, color, patterns and self-expression.

Learning is not *talking*, it is *doing*. Unless these children are involved with all their senses they are apt to lose interest. They go right on learning, but they may be learning such things as how to tune out, to withdraw, or to move the attention of the class to themselves, even if it is for a brief interval of some type of punishment.

As teachers we sometimes think of ourselves as people who teach reading and numbers, but telling is not always teaching. Teaching is a performing art. The process of learning is not just logical, it is sensual. We may get by with just logic for a right-side dominant person, but there are enough of the others around to interfere with classroom discipline. Then we are left with no rationalizations except to say that some children are immature, have short attention spans and are hard to motivate.

It is up to us to see to it that the stimuli we present have personal meaning. We must bring the real world into the classroom. We can let the children *do* something, and then see if we can help them generate a personal reaction which can be written down. There is no love in workbooks, and no personal meaning in a sentence made up by the teacher and copied off the chalkboard by the children.

As I have watched skilled, successful teachers interacting with dyslexic children I find that these similarities exist:

1. Much of the time it seems that there is satisfaction in the process of learning, in the things that are being done, as well as a feeling of success in the result of the actions.

2. Instead of discrete lessons there is an ongoing process, from which many projects spin off, come back together to be shared with the group, and then continued.

3. Each child seems to feel that he is making positive contributions to the ongoing progress of the group. There may be times when special arrangements must be made for hyperactivity, for inadequate ability to tune out distractions, or for frustrations with reversals, but these are treated as minor detours, with

the emphasis upon each child's important role in the group.

4. Instead of the teacher's voice being the thread that holds things together, there seems to be more discussion and more conversation going on with the children. I hear, "I don't understand what you are talking about." This is followed, not by the teacher explaining, but by various children explaining what they think is the thrust of the idea.

5. Instead of the teacher telling children what to do and following this by an explanation of what will be learned, I see children solving problems and discussing the reasons or results. There seem to be many choices of how to record findings, how to carry out projects and how to share results.

6. The teacher's role seems to be important in helping the children see how the learning is related to life outside the schoolroom, and to the needs of people, including the children.

The First Hour

The first remediation hour that a poor reader (or nonreader) spends with me is vitally important, for it sets the stage for the action which is to come. Many things have happened before that first hour of remediation. I have had a long talk with both of the parents. I have administered tests which will tell me many things I need to know, using a half-day to get acquainted with a person who is unable to cope with the learning situations which have come his way.

What have I found out? I know the level to which the reading, spelling and arithmetic skills have developed. Sometimes these levels are only pre-reading, pre-spelling and pre-arithmetic, but there is always a starting place indicated for me. I know the level at which the child functions on an individualized, standardized test of intelligence. I know the extent to which there are scrambling of letters or reversals of letters. I know if it is easier for this child to read aloud or to read silently, if there is enough reading taking place to make this judgment. I know the status of the child's visual-perceptual development. I know the lateral dominance of the hands, feet, eyes and ears. I know if spatial orientation is a factor to consider. Most important of all, I know something about how this child sees himself, and how he sees the world in which he lives.

After this evaluation I have had another long visit with the parents. I have shared with them the results of the tests which I have administered. I do not hold back any facts, for I do not want them to be passive bystanders in the process which is about to begin. I give a straightforward report, for that is what I would want if I were sitting where they are. I welcome all questions, but feel free to say that I do not know all the answers. If they do not understand, I try a different way of explaining. I show them the child's papers and I explain the purposes of the different tests. If they are sad about the limited achievement, I am sad with them, but only insofar as this sadness gives us an impetus to move on to ensure better achievement.

The most important part of this visit is to give, to my utmost ability, a picture of how the child sees himself and his world. There is an old proverb which says, "You don't know me until you have walked a mile in my sandals." I take the parents by the hand and help them walk that mile from the viewpoint of their child. There is great emphasis upon the idea that there is no value in trying to place blame on anyone. Probably every parent knows what it is like to go to bed feeling like a failure as a parent, and most of us do not get up the following morning intending to do a poor job of it again.

I put all the test results into writing, and I give this to the parents. I finish the report with practical, down-to-earth suggestions which I think will help the child. We discuss attitudes and approaches and strategies. Then we discuss the physical side of the question. There is no way to separate health from learning. Many of these children eat "junk food," and most of the parents know that it would be better if they did not do so. Now is the time to stop it. There is to be no "tapering off." The parents are instructed to go home and get rid of all food which has little to offer but carbohydrate. Carbohydrate is starch and sugar, and most children get far too much of it. We do not eliminate all carbohydrate, for fresh fruits and vegetables have carbohydrate, but they are also rich in other nutrients. We have an understanding that junk food is to be eliminated as conscientiously as would alcohol if the child were an alcoholic. It is often a real shock to the entire family to give up starch and sugar, but this is part of our agreement.

Many of the children I see do not get strenuous, daily exercise, and most of the parents know they should be getting it. They may have a vague feeling that the school is taking care of this, but it is too important to leave to guesswork. The parents agree to provide, and participate in, 30 minutes of strenuous exercise a day. Children will not take care of this themselves. The television is right there waiting to turn them into passive onlookers of life. Exercise must become a part of the regular routine for every member of the family. This too, is a part of our agreement. I do not want to work with flabby, undernourished children, and I shall be checking regularly to see if the parents are doing their part. A physician who has discovered that a child is a diabetic does not request that the parents try to watch a child's diet when it is convenient. He orders the diet and explains when or if exceptions can be made. I can do no less. I become a disturber of placid assumptions. I use all my persuasiveness to get a commitment from the parents that they will send me a child who is as healthy as good food and regular exercise will make him.

I do my utmost to depict what things are so stressful for the child that they must be eliminated if there is to be a chance for success. I explain that it is easy to gradually make the self-concept of a child more and more negative, but it takes care and planning to turn that child around to a path leading to positive feelings about himself. We talk about the negative aspects of the parents' self-concepts, and how these have stood in their way of fulfillment. We discuss the idea that no one wants to pass on these same negative feelings to a child. Now, they are ready to make some real changes, and I am ready to make my plans to see the child.

I have time to prepare. I must always have time to prepare. This is not a luxury; it is a necessity. The minutes with me must be productive ones. I get out all my notes and re-read them. I sit quietly and think about that child who came so trustingly to me to be tested. I think about how he looks when he feels inadequate. I try to remember any flashes of spirit. I think about the vulnerability of poor readers. I begin to feel that the child is trying to guide me. I relax and think about something which would bring a sparkle of interest and fun. I gather materials. I get extra ones, just in case I have misjudged. I feel myself becoming eager, and I know I am ready. I wish he would hurry up and come. I clear the room. There must be no pencils or books or chalkboard, for they are reminders of past failures.

Here he comes! His name is Mark, and he is eight years old. He is a "non-reader" but he can print his name, and he can count to twenty. He "hates" school, but he wishes very much that he could do well at the skills which are taught there.

"Hi Mark, I'm glad to see you. I have some things back here that I'd like to show you."

A wary look comes over his face. I wonder if he thinks it is a workbook for something hard to do. I hand him an egg, and ask him to break the shell so that the egg will be in the bowl I give him. He gives me an incredulous look and says, "You have to be kidding!" We both have a good laugh, and I ask him what he had expected.

"I thought you were going to make me read," he confesses.

"I'm not sure I can *make* anyone do that," I answer.

We get on with it. He asks me how to break the egg, and I tell him I am sure he can figure out a way, for an eggshell is not very hard. I sit there grinning at him, and break it he does, with most of the egg in the bowl, and only a little shell with it. I hand him an egg-beater and ask him to beat the egg. Again he says, "You have to be kidding!" This time I detect a tiny bit of courage in his voice. "Nope, not kidding," I answer.

I watch. This beating seems to be rather difficult for Mark. I wonder how many tools he has ever used. I make a mental note to bring a brace and bit next time to see if he notices the similarity. He is having trouble keeping the beater erect and turning the handle at the same time. What is he doing? He has changed hands! He is now holding the beater with his right hand and turning the beater with his left hand. He is coordinating his movements much better this way. But surely the turning of the beater requires more skill than holding the beater up. Now *there* is something I have never thought to measure: the dominant hand for turning an egg beater. Here is some more mixed dominance, for this "right-handed" boy, and I would never have spotted it if I had shown him how to hold the beater.

He is ready for the milk now. I show him where the milk is and let him get it. Again, I watch. He reaches in with his right hand and gets the milk, but he transfers it to his left hand. He uses his left foot to close the refrigerator door. I tell him he needs a cup of milk and hand him a measuring cup. I had hunted all over town for a measuring cup that was as large at the bottom as at the top, so that it would not tip over. I wonder who designs tippy measuring cups? He holds the cup with his right hand and pours the milk into it with his left hand. (More mixed dominance that I had not picked up on testing day.) This time he picks up the beater like a pro and turns the handle, left-handed, with confidence.

Fifteen minutes later we are eating flapjacks, and he is talking a blue streak. He is going to learn to flip them in the air. I suggest that it might be a good idea if we wrote down what he put in so that he could remember. He agrees, but says I can write and he will tell me what to say.

Out comes my old portable typewriter. "You mean I'm going to type? I can't type. You oughta know I can't type. How am I gonna type?"

After some discussion he says he will try to type just one part. He is going to say, "I busted a egg." I hold down the capital key and show him where the letter *I* is. He slams it down, looks up and sees that he has typed! I show him how to spell "busted," and he has already found the next "word" which is *a*. *Egg* is a fun one, with two *g's*. No one suggests that he give up his seat at the typewriter. His "recipe" reads like this:

I busted a egg. I splashed in milk. I put in the other stuff and got some on the hot pan and I flipped it and ate it and it was dam good.

Mark said he already knew how to spell "dam," because an older boy had taught him. He had known *two* words, his name and one more. Maybe some others will crop up, but they will not be in a school book, I think. We read his paper over several times. I tell him he is reading quite well. He stops dead in his tracks. "I can't read!" he yells. I look at him, grinning again.

Mark sits down, silent for once. I bring in a hole puncher and show him how to put holes in his paper and insert it in a notebook. He is still silent, and I wait. Then he looks at me and says, "How come I can read?" There is a little extra moisture in my eyes, but we both have a good laugh anyway. Mark walks out holding his notebook as if it were the Pulitzer Prize. I put my head down on my desk for a minute.

My cup runneth over.

One Lesson

I have often thought that it would be a fine thing if teachers could somehow find the time to keep a diary; a story of good days and not-so-good days. This should not be written to be funny, or to be entertainment for some future reader, but more as a record to go back over to learn more about the learning process. For many years, I was often anxious about the idea that there were so few hours in the week to "teach" all the things children needed to know. It was a little like the "Five Foot Bookshelf" which was supposed to make a learned, educated person of anyone who read all those words. I tried to sift through all the information which I thought was needed by children. At that time, knowledge must have seemed finite to me; my job was to choose the order and sequence in which to teach it, in hopes that each child would eventually get most of it packed away in little labeled boxes in the brain.

Now that teaching no longer seems to me to be a process by which I simply pass along all the "right" information, and seems more to be a personal relationship, much of my anxiety has left me. There are days when I am not at all sure that I have transferred any large amount of important information from my storehouse to those of children, but I do feel much more able to judge the quality of my relationships with them. Sometimes I have to charge myself with not having helped a student become perfectly clear about how he can divide fractions by fractions, but I am reassured if I can feel that during our mutual search for understanding and communication I maintained an open, rewarding relationship. I used to worry that children would have "gaps" in their learning; now I believe that everyone has these gaps, and whether or not the gaps are important will depend largely upon the kind of life that particular individual will lead. Besides, some of these gaps can be filled in quickly when one sees a need for them. When a young man decides to get a part-time job and borrow money to buy a car, I have found the teaching of multiplication of percents by dollars moves along at a rapid rate.

One of the interesting things about treating the student-teacher interaction as a personal relationship is the fact that somehow both the teacher and the student know when things are going well. This is true whether the student is there in a one-to-one situation or if there are many students in the room. In forsaking the premise that the primary function of a teacher is to gather and give out facts, I am not suggesting that the role of a teacher is to lounge around being a jolly, good pal while the children try to think up ways to make the day pass. Quite the contrary. In the role of a facilitator or helping adult, the responsibility to be knowledgeable and innovative is increased, in order that the relationship will continue to be a growing, satisfying one.

I have had some good days, even some very good days. I want to share one of them, even though the circumstances were such that another person could probably not repeat my experience exactly.

Nine-year-old Randy came to me as a "non-reader." He could print his first name when he wanted to, and he knew what a stop sign meant when he saw one beside the road. That was about all. One day we were looking for a folding ruler in a storeroom behind the building where my office is located. A large black spider was disturbed by us and made a random leap which looked very much like an attack to Randy. He screamed, "I *hate* spiders!" He took a swat at it, but it was too quick for him and escaped. The folding ruler no longer seemed very interesting, and we sat talking about spiders. I mentioned that spiders can see only about four inches, and that the spider really could not have been attacking us, for it could not see us. Randy asked me how much four inches was. This was the first "intellectual" question he had ever asked me, and I quietly controlled my excitement over finding something he wanted to know. We found the ruler, and talked about what it would be like to be able to see only things which were four inches or less away. Randy told me that the spider we had seen was a Black Widow, and it would kill us if it could. I suggested that we might be very, very careful and find out. Randy spotted the spider, and I carefully turned it over with my pencil to show him there was no red spot on the abdomen. Someone had left a glass half full of water in a corner, and we used it to magnify the spider so that we could see it much better than we could without magnification. Randy was entranced, and I was delighted, for I had seen nothing but apathy from him before.

Randy then thought he would like to catch the spider and take it home, but I asked him if he wouldn't prefer to see if it would spin a web if we left it there. I explained that this spider would only spin at night, and Randy suggested that if we closed the door and made it dark in there the spider might think it was night. We did this, but the poor harassed spider still hovered in the corner. I was able to make a special arrangement to get Randy to come to my office early the next morning, before school, and before my appointments began.

We arrived at the same time, unlocked the storage room, and found a beautiful web, intricately strung out over the tools and boxes. What a lovely, delicate thing it was, with the rays of sun picking up the strands of silken strength! We just stood there together, and Randy reached over and held my hand. Again, we sat down to talk. I told him that we now knew it was a female, for only the female spider can spin a web. This web had evenly spaced spokes going out from a hub in the center. I asked Randy if he knew that spiders cannot chew, but can only eat soup? They suck the soup out of bugs, I told him, and then tie up the dried-up, left-over part of the insect and drop it off the web. We talked about how spiders catch an insect, and Randy asked me how they kept from getting caught in their own webs. We went slowly into the office, now talking about how we are frightened of many things we don't know much about. I asked him if he would like to draw or write any- thing, and he said he would. I did not expect much from this little boy, but wow! He drew a large grinning spider eating soup out of a bowl, and then asked me how to spell "Bug Soup." I spelled it out on the felt board and let him type "Bug Soup" on his picture. Now Randy could read! He could read two words.

No, Randy did not immediately drop all his feelings of discouragement and swing right into being an eager learner, but he did make a start that day. I have never been able to repeat this experience for another student, but I think this day helped me sharpen my perceptions and increase my efforts to find innately interesting learning experiences. Who started that old myth that all worthwhile learning is hard and disagreeable? It seems quite the opposite to me.

How I Teach the Writing
of Letters and Words

I *start* the teaching of writing by giving the child something interesting to do which I hope he will want to write *about*. In order to write, it is necessary to know something about the shapes of letters. Many dyslexic children seem unable to learn letter shapes by looking at them. Perhaps this is difficult for everyone, but some learn it easier than others. Try this: get a book with Japanese letters (characters) and look at them. How many can you learn by just looking at them?

How do children *feel* the way to make letters? I like to start with something beautiful. I have a box of beautiful, smooth, large wooden letters, and they can be arranged on a table, on the floor, or on a shelf. They can be put down flat or made to stand up. If a child can sing the alphabet song, she often begins to sing and tries to put the letters in order. Sometimes she has trouble with the "l m n o p," which is often sung as if it were one letter. When interest in this begins to lag, I may hand her the capital letter which starts her name. As we work together, I give the sounds of the letters, but I do not ruin the procedure by drilling, over and over. I identify the letters by giving their sounds more often than I do by giving the names of the letters.

After we have spelled out her first name, if the interest level is still high, we may go on to her last name. If she is still eager, I may bring out a set of aluminum letters which look like brushed silver. They came from a hardware store and are meant for mailboxes, but they feel so cool and smooth that they are fine for spelling out words. I provide an experience worth writing about, and these two-inch metal letters are fine for spelling out, "I listened to a shell." If that is too much, we may just work on spelling "shell." "I held a toad" may be too much, so try just "toad."

On the market you will find sets of sandpaper letters. I don't like them. How could anyone ask a little child to run his fingers over sandpaper? The first time I tried it, I could not even finish the first letter. Wallpaper stores now have rolls of velvet paper with adhesive backing. Make your own set. If a child would like to have a set, let him choose a color from samples you have. Red velvet will be the favorite, I think. Imagine having a set of red velvet letters! (Would you rather have sandpaper?)

If you are making sets of letters, make them so that you can trace your finger over the letters in one movement. The standard alphabet is made with straight lines, circles and parts of circles, but dyslexic children often find it extremely difficult to hook together the parts of the lower-case *a*, *b*, *d*, *g* and *p*; make these so they can be traced in one movement. The *a*, the *d* and the *g* will be very much like cursive letters.

Start at the *x* and go in the direction of the arrow.

The *b*, the *p* and the *g* will also be made so they can be traced in one movement, starting at the top:

Follow this same principle for the *m*, *n*, *h*, *w* and *y*.

I avoid drilling on sounds and shapes of letters except when the child needs those letters. Once she starts writing, she will need more and more letters, and we use the sounds and shapes of them as the occasion demands. I have several sets of the cardboard letters, and I find them useful because one side is shiny and brightly colored, while the "wrong" side is "ugly gray." As one little girl said, "No one would use the ugly gray."

Children can help make letters from pipe cleaners, but this can be tedious, so do not be afraid to stop the project or to help when the interest is gone.

After a child has spelled important words with letter sets, he is usually ready to put some on paper. I like to start with a very large 16 x 22-inch tablet, the kind sold at office supply stores. A large felt marker can be grasped to make gorgeous letters, each one a different color, if the child desires. After he makes a satisfactory letter, try not to get in a hurry to teach more letters. Let him play. Show him how to make "fat letters."

Think back and remember all the different ways you made letters when no one was looking. Did you make letters by making continuous loops of ovals? When you were doodling at the phone during a boring conversation did you make letters with sloping lines which fanned out to go around a curve? Did you make dots or stars to decorate your letters? If you had felt pens did you write *green* with a green pen and *red* with a red pen? Did you write the word *ghost* with shaky, scared-looking letters? Did you make your words walk around the edge of the page? Did you ever write the word *mountain* by making it go up a hill and down on the other side? Did you write your teacher's name in prissy, prim dots, and follow it with your own name in strong, bold letters leaning forward? Did you make your letters with faces on them? Did you write, "I'm sorry," with saggy letters that had tears dripping down from them? Did you secretly write, "Get off my back!" starting with very small letters which got larger and larger until the last letter was huge and loud-looking?

If you give a child a little encouragement, he will find that making letters can be great fun, rather than dull drill. For an assignment, ask him to see how many ways he can write the word *no*. It can have a question mark after it or an exclamation mark, or it can be in different colors, or it can have decorations around it. After the letters are made, the vacant spaces can be filled in.

How about a homework assignment asking a child to bring in his name colored or printed in as many ways as possible? Or how about the three initials of his name made into a monogram? Did you ever make up a sentence such as "I am getting dizzy going around and around and around and around this paper." Did you start in the middle and spiral the words around in increasingly large circles? Isn't that better than drilling on how to spell *around*?

Did you ever stop to think that writing neat letters between two pale blue lines could be very boring?

One of the most delightful characteristics of the American version of the English language is that it changes constantly. If we do not have a word which fits, we make up one. Usually the new, improved words are started by the young people. The very first time a young person said, "Stop bugging me!" the recipient knew exactly what was meant. No one had to guess the meaning when the first young person asked, "Why are you so up-tight?" One of the most recent words which is widely used (but not defined in any dictionary) is the word *humongus*. The first time a child asked me how to spell that word, I not only knew how it should be spelled, I knew what it meant. I still remember his sentence, which was, "Last night after I got in bed I saw a great, *humongus* cockroach on the ceiling right over my head." Do you think I should have explained to that child that there is no such word as *humongus*? Just what word could I have substituted?

When a child is recording an experience which I have provided, there are very often words used which would not be found in a dictionary. Stop those words and you stifle any attempt to express what that child felt, heard or thought. If something *bammed* into him, that is what should be written. If he says the water *gurbled* out, that is what he should be helped to put down. Formality has no place in the teaching of beginning reading and writing. Often schools spend years removing all spontaneity from writing, until the students get to college. Then they are told to take a course in creative writing, and the teacher bewails their stilted, uncreative writing!

If he does not like to write, there may be a reason. Perhaps he could hold a pencil and punch a typewriter key instead.

Many dyslexic children are ready to begin to record ideas and feelings long before they are ready to write with a pencil or a pen. How about a typewriter? I have many very young children who can type faster than their contemporaries can write. I am not speaking of "blind" typing or typing by putting the fingers upon the "correct" keys. That can come later. My children punch a key which has a capital letter on it, and then look up to see what they have typed. Each time they do this they are connecting the shape of the easy capital letters with the more difficult lower case letters. They often surprise themselves and their teachers and their parents by memorizing most of the keyboard in a few short sessions. Some of them cannot hit the right keys with their fingers, so I give them an eraser which is shaped like a pencil. They can grasp this and come straight down upon the keys, fairly accurately. They are taught to respect the typewriter as a useful machine, which is never to be abused. However, abuse might come from unsatisfied curiosity, and I show them how the keys work, how to clean the keys, how to open up the hood of the typewriter to see what makes it work, and how to put a ribbon on. The back-spacer and the margin release are shown as soon as the need arises or as soon as they want to know.

When I bring out the typewriter, I do not expect a child to sit down and work alone. I help. When? I help whenever I am needed. I use eraseable paper, liquid paper, and corrector-tape. *I* do the erasing, the back-spacing and the painting out of mistakes. I continue to do this so that we can get on with the job at hand. I do the correcting until a child begins to think that correcting looks like fun and asks to be allowed to do it. After that, I still do most of it, and I always do it if the child seems to be impatient with himself when he makes mistakes. If he feels ashamed of making mistakes, I sometimes say, "Just think, if no one made mistakes, all the people who work in factories making erasers would be out of a job." Or I remind him that the last time I dropped the box of felt markers he helped me pick them up, or he helped me mop up the water I spilled. Turnabout is fair play. I make the point that I would rather help others correct their mistakes than to correct my own, and he can "pass it along." The next time he helps me do something, I remind him that he has "passed it along."

Why do I go to all this trouble? Typing can be a frustrating activity; I have personally typed the word *the* as many as three times, making the same mistakes each time. If a child is expected to turn out a perfect paper alone, the value of typing is lost. But all of this is part of the whole philosophy of not diminishing a child. Mistakes are diminishing if they are treated as character flaws. "What's the big deal?" as our young people have taught us to say. The object of typing for children is to provide an easy, quick way to communicate, and it does, with a little help.

What Can Children Write About?

Children, like adults, do best when they write about things they know, or things they are interested in and can find out about. Where shall we start? Let's start with the child and work on recording all the factual information possible. All of us are interested in names and ages. Listen to someone getting acquainted with a child, and you will probably hear, "What is your name? How old are you?" That is a good place to start.

Obtain a snapshot of the child and help her fasten it to the first sheet of paper that is going to be a notebook. Under this, help her type or print, "My name is_____." Next may come the age, and for a child who is old enough to grasp the many divisions of time which we have, the age may be figured in years, months, weeks and days. Then, see if you can find out what other personal measurements are interesting to the child. Most will include weight and height. Working with at least two people, this is a good time to show that if the measure on the top of the head is not exactly parallel with the floor, the height will not be accurate. How can you be sure it is parallel? Can you use a book next to the wall? Would a carpenter's level be better?

If the carpenter's level distracts all the attention, and the interest shifts to finding out how many things are even on top, so much the better. Take a fresh sheet and help her record all the things that are level on top and how many things are not. Could you make a level with a small, straight-sided bottle? Fine. Help her record how it was made, and to draw a picture of it, labeling all the entities.

We have still not found out nearly enough about the measurements of the child. What about the pulse? How does a nurse find a pulse in your wrist? How can you tell how many times your heart beats each minute? Can we use a second hand of a watch? Why would a stopwatch be better? A good assignment would be to find out how fast the heart beats for each member of the family. Friends can be measured too. If the interest remains high, measure how many times the heart beats after running around the building, or after jogging in place. If you merely write down all these numbers, you will not be able to remember what they are for. See what the child thinks should go with each number to be sure it will be remembered correctly.

If the interest in the pulse leads to an interest in the heart, fine. You may not have all the pictures and materials you need, but do the best you can and bring more the next time. When I asked all the children in a second grade class what the heart is for, some thought it helped them breathe, one said it gave you cancer if you smoked, some thought it digested food, and the rest did not know. It was not in the curriculum! That very personal little pump, which works away for each of us, day and night, asleep or awake, was unknown to all of them. I find that rather sad.

A good assignment might be to hold a pet such as a dog or cat or gerbil or guinea pig, and feel gently to see if the heart beat can be counted. Instead of those field trips each year to the fire station, maybe a few children at a time could go to a blood bank to see the wonderful process of donating blood. With the right preparation, those children will be counting the days until they are old enough to donate. For some reason, adults get queasy having children watch such an interesting event, even though those same children see blood and violence on TV as soon as they are old enough to stay up past eight o'clock.

We are not through with the personal measurements. Chest expansion is a good one. Show them how to take a deep breath and then let all the air out of the lungs. Measure quickly, while the chest is as small as possible. Help them record this. Then show them how to make the chest as large as possible, and record this. The chest expansion is the difference between the two numbers. You will be dealing in fractions of an inch, and what if fractions are not yet on the curriculum? Go right ahead and deal with them. I am often surprised at how easily fractions can be mastered when the information is highly personal, and therefore, important.

Measurements of physical feats can be done in small spaces if necessary. If she is lying on her back, how long can she keep her heels just one inch off the floor? Record this, for practice helps, and she may do better the next time. Almost any door can accommodate a chinning bar, and it can be used for other feats than just chinning. Hoist one child up with his chin up over the bar, and see how many seconds he can stay there. Put a chair under it and let him reach up to the bar. Remove the chair and see how long he can hang there without touching the sides of the door. Can she lie on her back and push up into a backbend? How long can she stay there? Practice helps, so she will need to write down the number of seconds to see if she can beat her record the next time.

When she gets through with all the timing, you will have had a fine chance to show her how many seconds make a minute, a half-minute and a quarter of a minute. Isn't it handy that there are the same number of minutes in an hour that there are seconds in a minute? (One seven-year-old was mystified about our timing and asking, "If there are always sixty minutes in an hour, how come some hours are so much longer than others?")

If interest in personal measurements wanes, provide personal experiences. Show them how to make something happen. Try not to do it yourself. Try to think of a way to provide the materials and suggest safe ways to use them. Encourage record keeping. Encourage drawings, which will need to be labeled so that others can identify the important parts. Get a book of magic tricks and learn how to do them. Then help them learn. Get a book of science experiments and help them learn how to do them. Then have a discussion (not a lecture) about what happened and why.

When teaching dyslexic children there is much to be said for the kind of teaching which takes place when the apprentice system is in operation. Most of us use it occasionally in our day-to-day life, but we do not use it nearly enough, and it is conspicuous by its absence in most of our schools. This may be because it seems easier to teach by telling them by doing. The fallacy of this attitude lies in the fact that much of what is said is not learned. It is, on the other hand, almost impossible to keep from learning when we are doing something meaningful.

For inadequate reasons many people have delineated certain intrinsically interesting activities as being suitable for only one sex or the other. As a consequence, boys have been denied the pleasure of learning to cook (unless they were camping out) and girls have been denied the pleasures of working with many kinds of tools. When working with dyslexic children we will do well to examine our ideas about such things as sewing being a feminine pursuit and repairing a leaky faucet being masculine in nature. No teacher who always has new things to use, as well as to talk about, ever has to worry about boredom.

When we are working with tools, we are not so tempted to lecture as we are when we have no resources but voices. We are not tempted to ask a little girl to memorize the difference between a ball peen hammer and a claw hammer; if she is using them she will learn the difference because you will say the name of the hammer as she uses it. She will feel the cold, rounded end of the ball peen, and she will learn with her hands how the claw hammerhead curls around as it bifurcates. (That word is in the vocabulary of even small children who use tools with me, for there is no suitable synonym, and it is a fun word to know.)

If you are showing children how to use a Stillson wrench (first grade is not too early for this) you will not introduce the topic by handing out mimeographed sheets which say, "A Stillson wrench is a wrench having a jaw which moves through a collar pivoted loosely to the shaft, with the jaw tightening as pressure is applied to the handle." If you had never seen a Stillson, do you think you would know what it was by memorizing that definition? The name is important, and if you enjoy tools you will not refer to it as a "thingamabob."

There is another important area of writing which is often neglected, and that is feelings, emotions, desires, yearnings, delights and aspirations. Most of our important life-changing decisions are made because of emotions and feelings, yet very little is said or done about them in learning sessions which are planned for children, either at home or at school. Children often grow into adults who cannot describe their own feelings. It has been said that we cannot understand a feeling until we can describe it, and it is never too early to start. When a child comes to you looking angry or hurt or sad or excited or pleased, make sure that these important feelings are not ignored. The lesson you planned can wait, but the emotions cannot.

Say, "How do you feel?" Then really listen. Listen not as if you think it is funny, or as if you must moralize, or as if ugly emotions should be squelched, but as if you really care.

Bring a stethoscope and a stopwatch to school. There will be many interesting facts to record, to read and to discuss.

Dyslexic children are probably more sensitive to slights and rejection than other children; they have so much of it that they feel it when it is not intended. That does not keep it from hurting. As the listening or writing adult, we must strive for empathy, not sympathy. We must soak it up without being judgmental.

We do not need to take sides and assure the child that the teacher is a heartless wretch, nor do we need to question the accuracy of the child's report. Instead of saying, "That was a terrible thing for her to do," we can respond by saying, "Let me see if I have written it down just as you remember it." That does not mean that we are to show no emotion ourselves. Without condemning anyone we can say, "You must have had an awful day!" For some, and you will know which ones, a hug can be a silent expression of empathy. Words are wonderful, but they are not the only means of communication.

We can extend the interest in writing by using a camera. The best kind is the kind that develops each picture when it is taken. Save all the directions. Everybody can help by reading one part at a time, aloud. Help the child load the camera. This does not mean loading it for him while he watches, and it does not mean handing it to him and letting him do as he wishes. Try to find a position someplace in between those two extremes. After each picture is taken, help him print captions, names, dates, and anything else he things would be good to have under the picture. Stay with the first picture until it is all taken care of, rather than having many pictures taken in a sequence.

As you do more of it you will think of more ways to help a child enjoy writing about things which are close to him. The writing helps a child take more steps to increase the things he knows about.

You Are the Expert

The problems of a child who cannot read adequately are often compounded by the fact that parents and teachers are afraid they will make mistakes when they try to help. But we all make mistakes with children, all kinds of children, and we are always forgiven if we are seen as people who are trying to help. Many teachers feel inadequate because they have not had college courses or university degrees dealing with dyslexia. I know a secret; none of us had training in this when we began to be experts, because there *were* no courses being taught. Some worthwhile courses are being taught now; others are useless. We cannot wait around for a new generation of teachers who will know everything they need to know, and we cannot realistically expect all the present teachers and parents to pull up stakes and go back to school. The dyslexic children are here, right now; someone must deal with them today.

You have already taken an important first step. You have picked up this book to see if there are any sensible ideas which can help you. The next step is to try to analyze the difficulties which one individual child is having. They are all different, and if you care about one child you may well be the only one who is doing any constructive thinking about what can be done.

You are the expert! Try to pinpoint what you want that one child to learn. "I want him to learn to read," is not specific enough. If his eyesight is unimpaired he can probably already read some. When he sees a stop sign he may know that it means that cars are supposed to stop, and he may be able to pick out his name from a set of cards with names printed on them. If he can do that, he is already able to see and interpret words a little. Basically, if he sees you draw a line, and can then draw one somewhat like yours, or can make something which looks a little like a circle when you do, he is already part of the way down

87

the road to writing. He has been learning a little. You must start where he is, and learn to set priorities in a way which will help him get through the days with as little damage as possible to his self-esteem.

One of the reasons we want each child to learn to read is to give each child the opportunity to learn a wide variety of facts which we, in our best judgment, see as useful, or interesting, or important. With the explosion of knowledge in the last century, there is no way we can hope to teach all children all there is to know about an infinite number of topics, so it behooves us to choose well, with great care, the facts and ideas which we feel will be the most useful or the most gratifying to a child who will grow to adulthood changed by our choices.

If you are a classroom teacher you may have a limited number of choices about what facts can be used in your classes. If you are a parent you may have to settle for helping a child learn the facts which have been picked out by someone else as being the most important. But from whatever situation you are in, there are many different ways of helping a child learn.

In the first place, many of the ideas and facts which a child needs are in books. The child is a poor reader, and you plan to do what you can about that. In the meantime, do not sit helplessly by waiting for the reading to improve. *Read aloud!* That is such a simple idea that you may not feel it can be very important. Or are you afraid you may "spoil" a child by reading aloud? Nonsense! You would read to a blind child, and to supplement your reading you would probably hire a reader to read aloud when you could not do so. No, your child is not blind, but she cannot make sense out of the words which represent ideas on an intellectual level which is challenging. When you are eight or nine or ten years old you are not very interested in books which were written for six-year-olds. So, read aloud!

Read what? Read anything you both like. School is right there waiting tomorrow morning, so you can read some of the things in the textbooks, too. Get those textbooks. Do not let any regulation or rule or red tape stand in your way. Use all your ingenuity and charm and deviousness and *get those books!* You may feel that reading out of the National Geographic and looking at the pictures together would be more fun, but tomorrow the class is going to be expected to know the things that are in the textbooks, so get those books. Having copies of the textbooks may have to be a delicious little secret between the two of you, but your child is going to have a chance to be knowledgeable tomorrow when the teacher leads a discussion about the things in the textbooks. This can be the biggest support for self-image which you can ever give.

If your child has homework, see to it that each day that homework is completed. It does not matter what you think about the homework topics. The two of you cannot choose. If there is writing to be done, it must be in the child's handwriting, and there may be an inability to process information which must be read, understood, stored, and then selected to put on a particular line after a particular question. Just the mechanics of forming the letters and getting them in the right order may be a big ordeal, so *help*. How much should you help? As much as you need to, and as much as cannot be done alone.

But will he quit trying if you do all this? Of course not. You can both tell when enough skill and self-confidence has been learned, and then the help can be lessened. When a sprained ankle mends, no one needs to tell a child to throw away a crutch. It is more fun to do it without help, and you will always be testing, a little at a time, to see if the next step can be taken without you. How can you tell? I do not know, but you can find out if you care enough and stay alert.

Would you like a little more help from me? I shall gladly share with you some of the ideas which have worked for me, if you will pass this along, and share with a child those techniques which have worked with you.

Go to the library with your child at least once a week. Two or more books can be chosen; one which you will read aloud and one book which the child will try to read, with as much help from you as is needed. This may be a new idea, and there may be some poor choices at first. You may want to supplement the choices of your own. You will both get better at it. Children have an uncanny ability to pick out books which are about on their reading level, and to also pick out books about things they want to hear about.

When will you read and how much? I do not know, but you will experiment and find out when there is the most receptivity and when you are best able to marshall

89

your thoughts in a way to concentrate on what is being read. Adults do not fool kids when they read without thinking about what is being read. If you want it to be important, make it sound important when you read it.

All reading problems and all learning problems are intensified when the print is small and the words are close together. If you cannot accept this readily, I challenge you to sign up for a class to learn a new language. You will find that the newest, most widely used texts for learning a foreign language are printed in large type, with wide spaces between the lines and generous spaces between the words. Why? Because publishers have found that they can sell more textbooks of that kind, even for adults. Can we do less for children who are learning a new skill? Many public libraries now have large-print bookshelves, but unfortunately many of the books are purchased only for our growing leisure class of older people. There are always books on subjects such as "How to Raise Orchids in Your Spare Time" or "Crafts for Your Grandchildren's Gifts." Do your part to let your librarian know that you need books on the interest level of your child. Express interest in having a list of large-print books which you can take to the school for help in selection. The more adults you involve in this project, the better. Librarians do not want to buy books which are not going to be read, so make sure they are read.

If a poor reader is hyperactive, it may be caused by genetic make-up or by boredom (hard things are boring). There are physical changes which can be made in the environment which will reduce the agony of restless bodies which seem unable to relax. If left to their own devices children will rarely sit in chairs in straight lines or even in a semi-circle. They usually choose the floor if they feel there is not going to be disapproval for this preference. A child can quietly change positions many times if her turf is outlined by a piece of carpet on the floor rather than by a hard chair not much wider than her bottom. Flexible teachers often wind up with less chaos and less distraction when children are not expected to stay in their chairs. Watch the teacher! Teachers do not "sit down and shut up," and some do not expect children to do so. They may be open to your ideas for flexibility.

A hyperactive body becomes less driven if the child is allowed (nay, encouraged) to take strenuous, aerobic exercise regularly during the school day. How often? A perceptive teacher can tell how often she is being tuned out. That teacher can tell exactly when the wiggles begin. It is then time for some or all of the children to get five minutes to exercise. A jump rope is one of the best pieces of equipment, for a child can keep track of the progress made, it is equally good for boys or girls, and it can be done almost noiselessly, in the back of the room or in the hall. Signals can be worked out so that children or the teacher can request a change of the routine. A hyperactive child should probably never go longer than 45 minutes without strenuous exercise. Here is a good chance for the teacher to ask the children to come up with ideas for exercise which is strenuous enough to make them pant for breath, but quiet enough to be acceptable in a classroom.

Distractability or "short attention span" can be dealt with by making it possible for children to cut down on the stimuli which keep them from concentrating. This must be done in a spirit of helpfulness rather than in a punishing way, or even the best ideas in the world will be rejected by the children. Study carrels can be purchased or made by the parents of children who are having trouble, shutting out movement and color. These can be labeled, on the outside, "OFFICE," and everyone can understand that people sometimes need to go into an office to keep others from disturbing them. If a child needs to whisper when "silent" reading is supposed to be done, a neat little gadget called a Tokbak* can be used so that the whispers cannot be heard by anyone else. If noise is a problem, inexpensive headsets can be worn while it is important to concentrate. Of course, no child will want to wear or use any of these if they are seen as punishments for not paying attention, but a skilled teacher can explain that grownups use all these techniques to help them function better at their jobs.

What can kids do when noises are too loud or unpleasant? They can press their fingers on the outside of each ear. Teach them to do that when they are reading.

Good health is connected with learning. Adults who deal with children, whether they are parents or teachers or both, should take on the responsibility of making sure that while the children are in their care, they will not be stuffed with sugar and starch. You cannot run a Datsun on kerosene. Junk food depletes the body, and the brain is, in a very real sense, part of the body. The combined weight of teachers and parents can bring pressure in the right places to see to it that school lunches offer a piece of fruit instead of a cornstarch pudding for dessert. However, when adults are making sure that the children are getting nutritious food and strenuous exercise, they may be wordlessly telling children that, "When you are grown up like me you will not have to exercise or watch your diet. You can then be overweight and flabby like me." Children do still look to their parents and teachers as models, and they are more apt to copy what adults do than what they say. Are you a good model?

Avoid using criticism. If the child says he cannot learn something, respond with understanding and empathy to those feelings. Try something like, "You really don't seem to be able to learn it that way, so let's see if we can find another way which will be better for you. People do not all learn the same way." Notice the smallest bit of improvement and comment on it: "I think you are beginning to understand it."

As adults we do not like to be criticised or compared to other people who do things better than we do. Children feel the same way. If there is another member of the family or another child in the neighborhood who is an honor student, it does not help to bring that in. Telling a child she is lazy may convince her that her laziness is a personal attribute which accounts for her poor performance. In short, it may become a self-fulfilling prophesy. Telling a child that you are disappointed in him only adds feelings of guilt to his already negative opinion of himself. A discouraged, poorly achieving person needs to feel liked and wanted and important. This does not mean that we must accept poor academic achievement and do nothing about it. We must do everything we can about it, but we must do these things without blaming anyone or being judgmental.

Just as all reading problems are intensified if the print is small, all writing problems are intensified when the child is expected to make small letters and numbers. Try to forget about any artificial standard of how large writing should be for a child of any particular age. *You* are the expert, and if you find that the letters are better if they take up two spaces, or three, use that size. You can save paper some other way. The paper is wasted if it is not used in a way which will result in good learning. I see papers brought from school which have arithmetic problems so close together that after the child has worked the problem, no one can tell where one problem ends and another one begins.

Try to make each lesson interesting. That is such a simple suggestion that it is often forgotten. I visited in one classroom in which the children were studying the different kinds of leaves. Would you believe that there was not one leaf in the room? The children were memorizing the names of simple and composite leaves, and most of the names of the trees and shrubs did not even grow in their state. Within five blocks of the schoolroom were dozens of kinds of leaves, on trees and shrubs which they saw every day. Whether you are a teacher or a parent, get your dyslexic child out there in the real world. A child with a reading problem needs to have reading reinforced by touching, examining, hearing and smelling. In the case of the leaf assignment, what a chance was missed to have children crush a leaf, feel its texture, and smell it! A mature oak leaf is dry and scratchy; a ligustrum leaf is soft and aromatic, a leaf from a tomato vine has a pungent, moist smell, and who can forget how a cedar leaf smells? What fun to try to learn the names and classifications of leaves so well that even with a blindfold on each child can identify them! Try not to miss any chances to make your lessons come to life. When you are working with a child at home, look carefully at each assignment and try to think of some way to gather materials of some kind to flesh out the bare bones of the assignment. Even magazine pictures are better than nothing. Often a map can be used, and sometimes a child can make an example of something connected with the topic. This serves a double purpose, if you are the parent. It helps your child learn, and it tells the teacher that the child is trying. Teachers feel insecure and threatened when they think children are not trying.

There are two enormously productive and rewarding activities which have been almost entirely left out of the curriculum for the dyslexic child; gardening and cooking. There is no school or home too small for some sort of garden space and for some kinds of cooking. Gardeners and cooks need to read about their work, and they both need to record successes or experiences which did not turn out just the way they had planned. There is no such thing as a failure in gardening or cooking, for each experience whets the appetite to vary the method and try again. Gardening and cooking are extremely gratifying because the cook and the gardener perform creative acts which put "magic tricks" right out of the picture.

Dyslexic children sometimes seem to feel that they are always being unpleasantly acted upon by their environments. That feeling is not conducive to effort in academic pursuits. The cook and the gardener *know* that they can make things happen. They are valued and appreciated by everyone, and that brings about a positive change in the self-concept. People who are valued feel that they are capable, and capable people try harder to accomplish anything which they see as important. I cannot think of any math or communication skill which cannot be taught in connection with gardening and cooking.

Cooking provides many opportunities for first-hand learning, as well as for integrating writing, reading and arithmetic.

I do not mean that we should sneak around playing dirty tricks on children by making them use numbers and reading and writing by sugar-coating these skills with some cooking and gardening activities. Rather, I mean that we can add to our pleasure and productivity when we use all sorts of skills in connection with our cooking and gardening. We will use them because we need them. We *need* to know how to double a recipe or cut it in half. We need to know how to substitute ingredients we have for those we do not have. We need to know how to use the recipes of others by reading, and we need to know how to record our own.

When we garden we need to know about chemical sprays and fertilizers. We need to know about the seasons and the soil and the moisture. Each person will have a better experience if we can learn what others have done before us, and can learn to communicate about what we have done. Both sexes and all ages can enjoy these two activities.

When you are having difficulty teaching something to a dyslexic child it is extremely important to involve multiple senses and both sides of the brain. Most people use the left side of the brain for language and numbers; they use the right hemisphere for visual-spatial learning. The right hemisphere is also used for intuitive and holistic learning. Holistic learning takes place when a person is able to see an over-all picture instead of a mass of details. All the senses and both of the hemispheres are needed for cooking and gardening. Use both of these skills at every opportunity.

In order to learn well, it is necessary to become involved. It is possible to *watch* cooking and gardening without becoming involved, but it is not possible to cook or garden oneself without becoming involved. In order to get the full value out of these skills, remember that the student should be doing the actions. If anyone is just watching, it should be the adult.

How You Can Help

When compassionate people come in contact with dyslexic children they often react with a plea of "What can I do for this child? Tell me how to help!" Those of us who work in this field sometimes see this as such a complicated question that we want to explain that first, the child must be carefully tested so that a prescription can be written for remedial work. Then, we may add, there must be a team effort with teachers, family members and friends working together to provide the maximum help.

By this elaborate approach we often turn off the enthusiasm of one person who wants to help one child. If we are realistic we must admit that it is probably not possible, in the foreseeable future, to get even the severely handicapped children properly tested, much less to be sure that they have good remediation programs planned and carried out. I have come to believe that a handicapped child is very fortunate to have even one concerned adult ready to act; when there is one in evidence it behooves us to encourage that one, rather than to frighten the helper off by implying that it is better to do nothing than to proceed without an expert calling the shots.

Sometimes this concerned adult is more apt to take direct action than are the people who have heard of one or more remediation programs, and are looking for advice on which one to buy. Nearly all of these programs have something to offer, particularly if we believe in them, but all too often the child is put to work with visual-perceptual tasks or exercises which may *seem* to be related to the problems, but do not tackle the problems head-on. Let us take a single, fairly simple example; A child who is confusing a lower case *b* with a lower case *d*. Rather than involve the child in making squares, circles and triangles, which do seem to be somewhat related, why not go right at the problem?

97

Helping with Letters

To begin, when we are confronted by two ideas or shapes or sides or directions which are confused, we will get better results if we teach only one component rather than trying to plug away at showing how things are different. If you are working with *b* and *d* confusion you must make a choice as to which one to teach first. If the child's name contains one of these letters, choose that one. If both letters are in the name, choose the one in the child's first name. Otherwise choose the *d*, because there are so many approaches which are possible with the *d*. Teach the *d* as a cursive letter by using the techniques described in Chapter XIII. Make the letter in the air, in a sand tray, with chalk, with big and little felt markers, with lipstick or soap on the windows, and with a stick in the dirt outdoors. Get a chant going as you make it, using something like, "Around and up and down with a curl." (Or any other words which you think describe the movements you are making.) When the child can make pretty good *d*'s, keep the interest up by chanting "*d* is for dad, *d* is for darn, *d* is for dumbledum, *d* is for daddy-longlegs, *d* is for daschund and drippy and dry-your-hands." The sillier the words, the better.

Move from the *d* to the letter *a* (not to the *b*). You can chant, "Around and up and a curl."

Try to judge when the interest is dying out, and quit just before tedium sets in. Here is where you have a great advantage if you are working at home with just one child. You can quit when you are tired of it or when the child is becoming restless. The next time you have the time to help, review quickly the *d* and the *a*. Then, go to the numeral *9*. For some reason, dyslexic children, more than others, make a numeral *9* by starting at the bottom. This movement results in something which looks roughly like a *9* at first, but it usually disintegrates into a figure which looks more like a backwards *p* or like a sideways cursive *e*. So, use the same movement as you did for the cursive *a*, and finish it by going straight down, so that it makes a nine. The chant can be "Around, and up and *way* down."

There is one more letter which fits into this series, and that is the letter *g* which should also be made as a cursive letter by dyslexics. Start with the same movement as with the cursive *a* and finish by going down low and curling it up to make a *g*.

If this doesn't seem like much of a feat, think about the hundreds of children who continually mix up the *b* and the *d*.

If you have helped one child straighten this out, you have been a real friend. If you go over these for a minute or two each time you can help the child, he will begin to develop a "feel" for the movement of these letters. There will be a "muscle memory" which will make the letters automatic. For, of course, muscles do have a memory; after we learn to ride a bike our body muscles do not forget this skill, even if many years go by between bike rides.

When the child thoroughly knows the movements of the *a*, the *d*, the *g* and the *9*, then the printing of the letter *b* will seem to be an entirely different letter, and it is not apt to get tangled up with any other letter. If I seem to be making too much of a small concept it is because there are only 26 letters in our alphabet, and if children can develop a firm foundation in differentiating them they will avoid problems which may happen every day to a dyslexic child who reverses letters. Also, this is an example of focusing upon one specific learning problem instead of using exercises which may only seem to be related to it. When in doubt, isolate the problems and deal with them one at a time. Try not to drill, over and over, on anything. Drill without pleasure becomes tedious and thereby loses its power to teach.

Helping with the Sounds of Letters

If you are trying to teach a dyslexic child to read, you will of course explain that the letters have sounds which go with them. However, you may find that it is not sufficient to sound out the letters c-a-t and say *cat*. To add interest and to keep the attention where you want it, hand the child a soft, stuffed cat. As each letter is sounded, move her hand down the back of the cat. Three strokes on the kitten's back will sound out c-a-t, and then a final one for the word, *cat*. Just because this is well-received does not mean it should be dragged out for a long period, so that the child will groan at the next sight of that stuffed kitten. A parent can use this once each evening with better results than if an entire reading lesson at school is expended upon it.

99

When this first word of the "at" family is learned, introduce other real items. Outdoors, three swings of a bat can be done with the sounds b-a-t, with a final one for the whole word, *bat*. Throw the ball at the bat after the word is pronounced. Ask the child to print *bat* on the back side of the bat. This is a good time to correct the batting stance. These children have enough problems without having some coach tell them they are poor batters. Make sure he is standing sideways, not facing toward the pitcher. Show him how to flex his knees and stick his rump out. Make sure his hands are close together. If he does connect with the ball, it will sail.

There is a marvelous toy rat with real fur and wheels. As you push the rat forward several times the wheels wind up a spring inside, so that when you let the rat go he scoots across the table or floor with a satisfying scurry. A child will almost surely enjoy pushing three times to sound out r-a-t, with a final good, hard windup for the word, *rat*. Now, can you think of three movements that will serve to teach *sat* and *fat*? Of course you can, and great fun it can be, too.

You will work out your own ways, but I find that it always helps to use *things* rather than just pencils, paper and books. After a child has learned that many words that rhyme have the same letters in the endings, start collecting things which have the same endings. I have a shelf with shoe boxes full of rhyming words. Start with a clock, a block, a lock, a rock and a sock. Mix these items in with a star, a car and a jar, and see if your child can separate those that end alike. As he finds two that rhyme, he can type the words for a record of his work. You will find many pairs such as fork and cork, book and hook, and dog and frog. Try not to bring confusion into the game by using words which rhyme but are not spelled alike, such as bear and chair. Instead, use bear and pear (a plastic one). Try not to rely upon pictures; little toys are much better. Look for miniature objects, such as a tiny fork (doll size), rather than large items. Let the entire family contribute to the box; it's more fun that way. See how many things you can find that end in *ing*.

How to Use Body Memory

The body has a memory—use it. Try a personal illustration: Suppose you cannot find your car keys. You may begin by quickly looking where they are supposed to be, and then frantically looking where you remember finding them before when they were lost. You may even go back to all those places again. In psychological terms this is called *perseveration*, which means doing something unproductive over and over. When you realize that perseveration is fruitless you may make a conscious effort to calm yourself while at the same time reminding yourself that you are going to be late. (Dyslexic children engage in this kind of activity often.) At this point you may try to think when and where you were when you last had your keys. The "thinking" is probably going to be a recalling of removing the keys from your car as a start, but I think you will find that you are remembering the feel of the keys in your right hand and the opening of the car door with your left hand. Your body may then recall putting an attached key into the house lock, setting down the things you were carrying, and perhaps answering a phone that was ringing, and then some other actions in a sequence. You probably will not think of these actions as if they were in word form; there is a more subtle form of remembering. Your body remembers; you retrace your movements as if you were doing them again. There may be no words involved at all, unless you are verbalizing for the benefit of another person. When you remember where the keys are, it is not a process of logical deduction, but is instead a process of calling into consciousness the experiences which were wordless. This is the process which we can use to great advantage with children who are having problems learning or retaining knowledge.

If you have a foolproof method for not misplacing car keys, try to think how you would find your way out of a wilderness if you were lost. Dyslexic people are often spatially disoriented, and ordinary streets may comprise a wilderness to them. Did you have a compass when you were a child? Did someone show you how to look in the direction in which the needle was pointing and then face north? Were you then shown that directly behind you was south, to your left was west, and to your right was east? Buy your child a compass, and help him learn to use it. Do some beginning map training. When you go someplace in the car, ask him to check and see which direction you are going. Keep a map on the car seat and pull over once in a while to locate where you are on the map. Work out ways between the two of you to keep yourselves straight with the compass. There will be times when it will seem to each of you that one of the directions is in the wrong place, so you will need to work on getting a body memory of facing north and knowing that south will be directly behind you. Sometimes it takes dyslexic children longer than other children to understand what it means to know what direction a road is going. Some go most of their lives without ever giving any thought to orienting themselves in the world by directions. What seems to come naturally to some people must be learned a step at a time by others. When teaching children to develop a sense of direction, try to adopt the frame of mind that you are helping them learn something which will be useful, rather than explaining that they have a poor sense of direction. A poor sense of direction is a relative concept; some rarely have it and some nearly always have it. It will not help to divulge the information that you have always had a good sense of direction, for this will give rise to a feeling of defeat.

While you are teaching the skill of map reading, pause a minute and decide where you think the four directions are. Do you mentally face north, or do you perhaps mentally move yourself toward the direction you know the sun rises? Try to sharpen up your consciousness of your body memory, and then try to introduce this kind of learning when you are working with a child with spatial problems.

Helping with Left and Right

Run a quick little test on your child. Ask her to touch her left elbow with her right hand. Is there a long pause? Hold your two hands out with the thumbs up. Ask her to touch your left thumb.

If this was not easy, or was incorrect, start with one concept at a time. Do not try to teach right and left together. Choose the hand she writes with. If this is her right hand, help her gain a strong feeling of which is her right foot, right hand, right eye, right knee, right ankle and right ear. With her cooperation, the buckle or shoestring of her right shoe can be marked with a red marker. Get her a ring for her right hand, and put a piece of elastic around her right knee for days when she is wearing long slacks. At home, put a rubber band around her right wrist; she may be able to remember how it feels even when it is not there, by using body memory. When there are pockets, put something in the right pocket, but keep the left one empty. Put a dab of cologne or after-shave lotion on the inside of the right wrist.

When a child can tell right on his own body he knows that the other side is the left side, so no drill is necessary. When he has his own body orientation straight he is ready to translate this to the body of someone facing him. Stand beside him, with a scarf tied to your right hand. Move over in front of him with your back to him and hold up your right hand. Mention that it is your right hand. Slowly turn around so that you are facing him, discussing what is happening. Then move back in front of him with your back to him. Repeat another day by tying a scarf to his right leg and to your right leg. Be patient. This concept takes time.

Helping with Reading

If you want to help with reading, read aloud to your child every day. This is such a simple idea that it is sometimes difficult for a teacher, parent, grandparent or friend to believe that it is important. Each time you are planning to read, go to the library and check out some books. What will be learned from this? Hundreds of things, but here are a few:

1. They can learn all the facts and ideas that the author had in mind when the book was written. I have been struck by the fact that I rarely read a book aloud that I do not need to stop and explain a new word or a new idea. Try not to hurry. Take time to look at the pictures and talk about them. Let the child do some of the talking. Ask her some questions about what she thinks the author meant. Of course, when the action is exciting you will not stop for a philosophical discussion. You will hurry fast, and you will let the excitement come into your voice. Practice reading just any book as if you feel the story is very interesting, or moving, or humorous.

2. They can learn that books are important to you. The way you hold a book, and the way you turn the pages teaches children more than a long lecture. You may say, "Let me wash

103

my hands first, before I read the book." This will be much more apt to be heeded than a lecture would be. When you find a book that has been marked in, let the child help you clean it up with an art gum eraser, gently going over the marks thoughtless people have put there. When you find a torn page, mend it neatly with the special book mending tape you will keep for this purpose. When you put the book away in a special place so that you can remember to return it to the library, this is apt to be copied too.

3. They can learn that a library is a good place to go for variety. You may want to voice the idea that none of us can own all the books we might need or want to use, and that is what libraries are for. Of course, we all have a few loved books that we want to own so that we can read them over many times, but children have a strong need for variety. "Why don't you go read a book?" is not a very interesting suggestion to a child who is tired of all the books in the house.

4. They can learn that you care about what goes into their minds, and about things that interest them.

5. They can learn that you are willing to admit that you do not know the answers to all questions, and may have to go look something up. They can learn that you may not know where a certain city is or where a river or a mountain is, and how you go about finding out.

6. They can gain a feeling of companionship with an adult that can be acquired no other way; both of you are together in an imaginary place, with imaginary problems to be resolved, or marvelous adventures to experience. The beauty of the words, and the music of the sentences may be more important than the plot itself. One eight-year-old boy told me, "I like it when my dad reads to me because

the words are slippery." We typed that sentence, and that father called me to say he had been very moved by such praise.

When and how and where will you read? You will get a feel for this. You will learn to stop before the interest lags, and to hurry through the parts that seem uninteresting. If you can "lie on your stomach" as the kids say, with the child beside you, you will keep interest longer. If you cannot manage that, sit on the floor and let the child lie down or sit up. Keep a plain, white card under the line you are reading so that the listener can follow what is being read. If you do it, the child will take it for granted that this is a good way to keep the place, and will not feel apologetic about using a marker when you are not there.

If the reading is easy enough, read a short paragraph in unison with your child. Keep a card under the line. This is sometimes called "choral reading." If you feel that a child has trouble keeping the place, look for books with large print. Speak to the librarian about lists of books which come in large print editions. Librarians like to order books which will be read; they will not know there is a need for large-print books unless you and others tell them.

All reading problems are intensified by small print. The conventional Bibles, dictionaries, encyclopedias and paperback books present a real problem. There are good dictionaries and encyclopedias in large print. Find them at the library or buy them. In general it is a good idea for dyslexic people to avoid small print books.

When reading is assigned for homework, take turns reading aloud. Stop at each page and ask a question about what has been read. Try to find what is the best way for your child to learn from the printed page. It is better to cover less material than to hurry through without understanding.

When you are reading aloud, tape your reading. This tape can be used for listening several times for important material.

After you have read a story, ask your listener to tell you what she can remember of the story. If the story is started in the middle, ask what happened before that. If she loses the thread of the story, open the book and help pick up the action so that she can go on. Later ask her to tell the story to someone else, using the pictures if necessary, to stay with the story.

When you begin to read aloud regularly you may find the child has more interest in reading aloud. Try to find a child at least two years younger and ask your child to read to her. Talk to the teacher at school and find out if your child can read aloud to one child in the kindergarten or first grade.

Take your turn, and listen while the child reads aloud to you. Really listen. Listen to see if what is being read makes sense, and listen for reversed letters and for scrambled letters. If the sentence with the word *felt* in it makes no sense, perhaps the word should have been *left*. If the sentence sounds a bit strange with the word *tea* in it, perhaps the author meant the word *eat*. Just go over quickly and say something such as this, "Oh, I see what the trouble is with that sentence. You got all the words right except this one. It should be *arm* (not *ram*)."

Can you see that the wording of this implies that there was something wrong with the sentence, not with the reader, and that the emphasis is on the fact that all the words were right except one? This is not supposed to be a tricky way to keep the young reader from having hurt feelings. It is supposed to be an honest expression of a desire to be helpful rather than derogatory.

If you are going to read aloud to a child and listen to that child read aloud to you, you will have to get two kinds of books, one kind which you will enjoy reading and he will enjoy hearing, and another kind which he is capable of reading aloud. For many dyslexic children there may be a wide spread of difference between the two kinds of books. When the two of you go to the library, make it clear that there are to be two different kinds of books taken home. Children become very adept at choosing books for the two categories.

What else can you do? You can look over the homework with him. You can spread it all out and help make a plan for getting it all finished. You can help. This does not mean that you settle down to do the homework while he wanders off to see what is on the TV schedule. It means that the two of you look it over and map out a plan for getting it all done in a reasonable length of time. It means that you stay right there if necessary, to see that things keep moving along. I have seen dyslexic children sent to their rooms and told that they cannot come out until all the homework is done. Even if the teacher assures you that the work is not too hard, you are going to have to make a decision about that yourself. He will not get it done by sitting in front of an open book and going into a coma. Even if you must read aloud most of the assigned work, send that child to school the next day with all that homework finished, and with every blank filled in. If he were blind, you would read to him so that he could get the meaning from the assigned work. He is not blind of course, but the handicap of dyslexia may be interfering so much that there is no meaning from the printed page. So help. How much? Feel your way on this. Keep encouraging him to do any part which you are pretty sure he can handle, but he should not have to spend hours each day after school on homework. He needs time for goofing off, for running and climbing, for playing with friends, and even for being quiet. No child should have a completely structured day. You be the judge.

When she has a paper or report to write, try to find material about famous dyslexics. Here are some suggestions:

> *Thomas Edison*
> *Alfred Einstein*
> *Michelangelo*
> *Leonardo da Vinci*
> *Luci Johnson*
> *Nelson Rockefeller*
> *Winston Churchill*
> *Susan Hampshire*

How can you help an older child? You can be a good listener and show that you care. You can be there to help him organize his time so that precious hours are not frittered away without anything to show for the time. You can help when others laugh or do not understand. You can read to him. If he were blind you would not quit reading to him when he left elementary school, and anyone who has an eye-tracking problem will always benefit from having someone to call on to read aloud when the eyes are tired and the temper is short. You can be a friend.

Helping with Math

There can be no real separation between words and numbers. Numbers can even be written as words, and words are used to describe real-life problems which require numbers to solve. All adults use numbers in their everyday life, in work and in play. Try to share your need for numbers with the child who is handicapped by inability to process symbols easily.

Some dyslexic children go to school many months without really understanding what *minus* or *subtract* means. Ask your child to help set the table. Then, ask him how many plates he used. Talk about how many places would be set if two people were not eating at home that day. Write that problem down in numbers. Ask him to bring you eight paper napkins. Ask how many would be left if three were taken away. Write this problem out the way his subtraction problems are written at school. Be as ingenious as possible, working with things that he sees at home. It is better to work on this for a few minutes every day than to spend several hours on the weekend. Work with marbles in muffin pans, with towels, with apples, with socks, with shoes and with anything else you can use around the house. Addition and subtraction are really two parts of the same process of making a quantity greater or smaller.

Get an abacus. If your child says that it is a kindergarten toy, tell her that they have been used by adults for many years, especially in the Orient. Be sure yours has ten wires, each with ten beads. One of your goals will be to help your child move away from counting everything up on her fingers. Help her learn to look at four beads and know how many there are without counting them. Move from there to recognizing five beads by grouping three beads together and two beads together, then four beads and one, then two beads and three. Help her find all the different ways of grouping numbers so that there will always be a total of six. When she can do this easily, move to grouping beads for adding. The next step is multiplying, which is really just a quick way of adding. Do this gradually; work a few minutes a day, beginning each lesson with a review of the last lesson. Stay relaxed and friendly. Quit when you find yourself getting tense.

Buy a stopwatch. Make sure it is used as a valuable tool—not as a toy. Keep it put away until he can think of a real use for it. Be ready with suggestions such as:

1. Record how long he can stand on his left foot, and then on his right.

2. Record how long he can hold his breath by holding his face under water.
3. Record how long he can stand on one foot with his eyes shut.
4. Record how long he can hold his arms out from his sides with the body still.
5. Record how long he can hold his feet six inches off the floor while lying on his back.

Save all these measurements in a notebook, and have him read them to you each time he wants to try to better his performance.

If the math papers have been messy and inadequate, find out from the teacher if your child can have the problems copied off in large numbers, with large spaces between the problems. Offer to do the copying. Some dyslexic children have trouble keeping their eyes on one set of numbers when the paper is covered with problems.

Find out from the teacher if she would be willing to put the marks that indicate errors on the paper with pencil rather than red ink. Get all the papers at the end of the week and work on correcting all the problems. When a discouraged child sees a paper covered with big red X's the temptation is to wad it up and get it out of sight. "Forgive" the mistakes when they have been corrected.

As a child gets older there will be more ways in which she can participate in the family finances. Pay her for balancing the family checkbook; she will benefit both by the math and by the understanding of where the money goes. If she is paid for any other work, let her figure up her own wages by the hour. When she wants to buy something, help her look up the prices in as many places as possible. If catalogues are used, figure in the postage. Help her figure up the gas mileage for the car.

As children become more involved in the day-to-day math of the family, math will not be seen as a "subject" at school, but as a necessary part of living. "I hate math!" is said when children do not see math as relevant to their lives.

How to Help Other People Understand

There will be times when it will be evident to you that other people do not understand that your child has a handicap, or how the handicap affects his academic performance. There will also be times when you are reluctant to step in because you do not want to appear to be a meddling, over-protective adult. On the other hand, you may be the only person with the knowledge and ability to interpret for the child. Certainly the child cannot do this.

How can you intercede without making the teacher defensive and irritated? Remember, school is her "turf," and she has spent many years and a great deal of effort becoming the expert. Nothing will be gained if you make her feel that you think she is incompetent or unkind. Children often sense this and plead with their parents not to go to the school, saying that they are in enough trouble already.

Just as there are times that we must try to walk in the sandals of the handicapped child, there are also times when we must try to put ourselves in the position of the teacher who has many other children who also need her attention. Besides trying to help individuals, each teacher has an overall responsibility to keep the discipline of the entire room within her control. When we have suggestions to offer, they must be offered with the knowledge that the teacher has a limited time to deal with one student at a time.

The suggestions you make will be made only when your individual child has a need for help, and not all dyslexics have the same needs. Here are some suggestions which I have seen accepted by teachers:

1. If the child is easily distracted it may be important to cut down on the stimuli which assault his senses in the classroom. Teachers like to keep their rooms interesting, and you will see plants, posters, children's art work, aquariums, mobiles and many other decorations in most classrooms. When the teacher thinks your child is not paying attention, it may be that she is really paying attention to a great many things, one of which may or may not be the teacher's voice or the book on the desk. Ask the teacher if you can contribute a study carrel to her room. A good one can be made from three pieces of plywood, hinged together. About four feet high is a good height, and the carrel should be wide

enough to fit around a desk. It should not be decorated, for that would add distraction. It should be hinged in such a way that it can be folded up and put away when the floor space is needed for other activities.

It should be placed with the middle section of the carrel against the wall with the open side toward the classroom. No one wants to go into a cubicle which is totally closed off from the other people in the room, but a child using a carrel can look over her shoulder and see the other children. Many teachers have found that putting a sticker saying "Office" on the outside is helpful. How it is used makes a great deal of difference. If it is used as a punishment because the work is not getting done, it becomes virtually useless. One skilled teacher introduced it in this way: "We are so pleased that Bill's father made us a study carrel. Many colleges have these so that students can work without being distracted by the other students. We shall call ours an office, and if other children are distracting you so that you cannot get your work done, raise your hand and when you catch my eye, point to the office. If I nod my head that means you may use the office. It may be that others will want to use it also, so I may have to limit your time. If I notice that other children are distracting you, I shall try to come back and whisper to you that you may use the office until you finish your paper." Can you see that this makes it a privilege to use the carrel?

2. Ask ahead of time about the teacher's policy of homework. See if it would be possible for your child's homework to be assigned in a special way. Ask the teacher to save all of your child's papers for the week and give them to you, sealed in a brown envelope, on Friday. Ask her to pencil in small x's where there are mistakes. These papers can be the homework for the weekend. Have a regular schedule for sitting with your child and help-

ing get these papers corrected. Some of them can be spontaneously corrected by your child. Try to avoid just telling the correct answer. Talk about the concept. Explain by using other examples. As each paper is corrected, let your child erase the x's and put it in a stack to return to the teacher. When they are returned, perhaps they can be marked by the teacher with a comment such as, "All corrected," or "Good work," or some other approving comment. What she puts in her grade book is her affair, but your child will have the satisfaction of having some perfect papers to keep.

3. If possible, your child's grades should be mailed to you, signed by you and mailed back to the teacher. Your child does not need to see them. A bad report card does not help a dyslexic child work harder. Be sure to provide the envelope and the postage for this mailing.

4. If your child has great difficulty copying material from the chalkboard, or even from other sheets of paper, without great stress, discuss with the teacher what the other ways are for her to get the important information she needs. It may be that you can pay to have it copied mechanically. If there is no copy machine, perhaps hand copies can be made. Offer to help. Only the teacher is in the position of knowing the best ways to handle this particular situation.

5. If your child seems unable to read silently, see if the teacher is willing for him to use a "Tokbak." This is a handy little gadget made by Developmental Learning Materials, whose address you can find in the principal's library of catalogues. It is a light blue piece of plastic which cups over a person's ear and extends over the mouth. Singers sometimes use them to hear how they sound when they are singing with a group. A child who cannot get much meaning from silently looking at words can

don one of these and whisper as he reads without disturbing others. The teacher may point out that this sort of reading is not as fast as what can be done by scanning a page silently, but some people are unable to scan. Whispering it may be slow, but it is better than not comprehending what is read. I have seen children raise their level of reading as much as two years when they have used a Tokbak. Again, if the teacher does not explain it as a useful tool and explain that others may want to use it, your child will object to using it. No child wants to be that different from his peers.

6. If sound is a distraction to your child, discuss this with the teacher. Earmuffs of the kind used by men who work at airports can be ordered from The Orvis Company in Manchester, Vermont. These will virtually eliminate all sound. They also have ear valves which can be used quite inconspicuously. Here, as always, the teacher's attitude can make all the difference. Do not buy them and instruct the teacher to see that they are used. Discuss it with her and ask if she will be willing to try them. Anything you do which antagonizes the teacher will work to the detriment of your child.

    Sometimes you will find a teacher who rejects any suggestions which are offered on the basis that it will interfere with her plans for the day. She may be concerned that someone in the administration will object to the changes. At a teacher's meeting I was told that they would like very much to use innovative teaching but they were sure that the administration would object. Later I met with a group of principals and curriculum coordinators who said that they would certainly like to see some of these new innovations used in the school, but they did not think the teachers would accept them! If you feel that one of your suggestions is not well accepted by the teacher, ask in a friendly way for a conference with the principal and all of the teachers or staff members who work with your child. I think you will find that the barriers fall quickly when everyone is there.

Teachers and school administrators are, in general, people who genuinely want children to learn. They are human and they have bad days, headaches and feelings of discouragement just as all of us do. Approach them in a friendly spirit of cooperation. If you look and listen you will be able to find something to praise and something to express your appreciation for. That makes a good beginning for a meeting. The school may not have a fund for buying plywood to see if a study carrel is useful. It is appropriate for you to offer to make it or to buy a ready-made one from one of the equipment catalogues which the principal has. The teacher might prefer to start with a large cardboard box with one side cut out. Maintain an attitude of flexibility and trust. Like Charlie Brown; your child needs all the friends he can get.

EPILOGUE

The Truth Shall Set Me Free

Now you shall know the awful truth, and perhaps the telling of it shall set me free. I am a dyslexic. (There is no such thing as a "former dyslexic.") Somehow I taught myself to read, I made my compensations, and I am halfway convinced that I would never have learned how to read if I had waited for a school to teach me.

I have lived a secretive life, always watching for signs that someone is *finding out*. As a child I did not know what the name of my condition was, but I was sure that I would be avoided like the plague if and when the truth was leaked. I knew that in my state of Louisiana there were people called lepers who had been banished forever by their families and sent to a special place to a living death. I did not think I was a leper, but I felt sure that I would be forever separated from normal people when others found out about me.

I stoically hid all symptoms of illness for fear that someone would examine me and find out something dreadful. This started when I was asked to open my mouth so a nurse could look into me. She looked, and said in a cold, disapproving tone, "Her tongue is coated." A cold hand squeezed my insides. Here it was! My mouth snapped shut and nothing could induce me to show my coated tongue again. They pressed my jaws; they inserted a spoon handle between my protruding upper teeth and my lower teeth, but my mouth stayed shut. My strength was as the strength of ten, but not because my heart was pure. That coated tongue would never again be seen by THEM. If they found out, it would not be by my coated tongue.

There were always lurking dangers which threatened to expose me. I could not learn to tell time. Miss Washburn stood over me, glaring with unconcealed contempt. She aimed that long wooden pointer at the big fake clock on the wall. The tip came to rest on the number 1. "Five!" she said between tight lips. "It's *five* minutes after nine." The tip of the pointer moved the clock hand to the number 2. "Ten! It's *ten* minutes past nine. What's the matter with you? Can't you understand anything?" In my fantasy world I could become invisible. I had only to double up my toes, suck in my buttocks and stomach, push my elbows hard into my sides, and "poof," I had evaporated. "Stop looking like that!" she yelled, and the stinging pain on my ear told me I had not disappeared after all.

I could not remember my birth date. As a matter of fact, I did not know what a birth date meant. It was not something I could ask about because the rest of the world obviously knew all about it. Teachers seemed always to be asking me to write down the date of my birth. Eventually I came to understand that this happened mostly at the beginning of the school year, or when I was taken out of one class and put into a lower one or a higher one, which happened often. I learned to cope with this question after a fashion. Each morning I asked one of my parents what the date of my birth was. They said, "November 17, 1917." I repeated this over and over until I could get into the family bathroom and lock the door. Once locked in, I pulled down the top of my black bloomers and wrote that seemingly important date on my belly. Now I had it. When I reached the school playground I had an uncanny ability to tell when I had about two minutes before the bell rang. I dashed to the girl's toilet room, held my breath so I would not have to smell the nauseous odor of that horrid place, pulled down the top of my bloomers, and copied my birth date into the palm of my hand. I kept this hand tightly closed to protect the date written there until I could find out whether or not I would need it that day. I still get a quick little chill when I am faced with a form to fill out and see the words "Date of Birth" taunting me.

I could not remember on which side of the page I was supposed to begin my writing. We had tablets of grayish paper issued to us by the state in those depression days, and they were strictly rationed. Sometimes I had to write all my work over because I had written from right to left instead of left to right. Then I ran out of paper, and that was a serious misdemeanor.

Miss Kidd would smile as best she could and say, "Now Anita, remember, we start at the *left* side of our papers, don't we?" I would glance furtively at Angela who sat next to me with her pencil all poised to write, and I would put my pencil at what, I sincerely hoped, was the left side of my paper. Miss Kidd would come by to check me and say, "That's *right*, Anita." Right? Did she say *right*? Oh dear God, I was so sure it was the left, but it must not be, so I moved to the other side and wrote my spelling in what I now know was "mirror writing."

When Miss Kidd picked up my paper her calm would desert her. Her theory was that all that unreadable writing was caused by the fact that I wrote with the wrong hand. Out came her ruler, and she vented her frustration upon my left hand until the blisters came and then broke. I never cried and that seemed to make it worse. "You are an unnatural child. I'll make that hand so sore it can't hold a pencil. The prisons are full of left-handed people." She was my first experience with "behavior modification."

I wet the bed. I slept on an old army cot, and several nights a week I soaked it. I pretended I did not know that the cot and I were wet. I never spoke of it, and it was never mentioned to me.

In some unexplainable way I felt sure that my wet bed was part of the whole nasty secret of my being different. The black bloomers were part of it too, and were part of my punishment for being sub-human. Certain phrases stuck in my mind, for I was an accomplished listener-at-doors-and-open-windows. In second grade I sat outside the principal's open window, hidden in the crepe myrtle bush, and heard Miss Cunningham say, "There is something strange about Anita. Sometimes I think she is not right in her head. I do try to be patient with her."

I was sure she was right about my head, for it hurt most dreadfully some of the time. My legs cramped at night too, and since no one else had leg cramps, I added this to the big mess that I had turned out to be. When my head hurt I often had dreams of it bursting open, spilling blood and pus all over everyone, to my complete humiliation. My dreams were not all bad, however. There was one beautiful one in which I flew. I soared and drifted in neatly banked circles. I swooped downward at full speed. At the last second I caught a current of air and rose effortlessly upward, glancing victoriously at my schoolmates and teachers who were watching me with awe. At about that point I usually fell out of bed and had to crawl ignominiously back onto my canvas cot.

In fifth grade Miss Rogers spent a great deal of time on geography. I was in deep trouble. Not only could I not learn which countries were "bounded by" others—I had no idea at all of what a map meant. She had a large number of maps on an easel-type apparatus. They were fastened together at the top and she could flip them forth and back during her lectures on geography. I could see that these maps had shapes with names of countries on them, but I could not visualize a country which stood up in the air and rested upon another country at its bottom. I had my own fantasies, but even I could not dream up places thin as paper which stood perpendicular to the ground. When, as an adult, I took my first trip on a plane, I looked out of the window and saw below me, a map! It looked much like those shapes on the maps on the fifth-grade easel, and for the first time I had a *feeling* that I understood what a map was.

So now you know. My family and friends often laugh at the routes I choose to drive. It was a wonderfully strengthening experience for me when I found out that many highly intelligent people are "spatially disoriented." If only I had known some good, solid words like "spatially disoriented" when I was growing up, what a difference it would have made!

I cannot remember the year I graduated from college, the date of my marriage, the years my children were born, the year I had an appendectomy, nor any of the dates which I am periodically asked to provide. When a physician asks me for dates I answer quickly with just any old date so he won't *find out*. There are conflicting dates about me in files all across the country, but apparently no one cross-checks such things.

The children come one-by-one into my office and into my life. I see the furtive, trapped look when a child is wondering if I will *find out*. I think of the tell-tale burning of my face, and the sick feeling I have when someone tells a "funny" story about me. I reach out to that child and hope he does not want to disappear.

When people ask me how I know a child is dyslexic, I laugh inside and try to give them an answer which will mean something to them. How do I really know? Does a pickpocket know another pickpocket? I know all right, for it takes one to know one.

If this book has seemed long on feelings and short on logic, you now know why. If it is deficient on sequencing and loosely organized, remember that it was written by a left-handed, weakly-lateralized dyslexic with mixed eye-dominance.

BIBLIOGRAPHY

1. Griffiths, Anita N., "Academic Achievement of Dyslexic Children During the First Twelve Months After Intensive Remediation," *Florida Scientist*, 31:1, Winter, 1973, 78-84.

2. Griffiths, Anita N., "Dyslexia: Symptoms and Remediation Results," *Quarterly Journal of the Florida Academy of Sciences*, 33:1, March, 1970, 1-16.

3. Griffiths, Anita N., "Leave Dyslexics in the Classroom," *Academic Therapy*, VIII:1, 57-65.

4. Griffiths, Anita N., "Self-Concept in Remedial Work with Dyslexic Children," *Academic Therapy*, VI:2, Winter, 1970-71, 125-133.

5. Griffiths, Anita N., "Self-Concepts of Dyslexic Children," *Academic Therapy*, XI, 83-90.

6. Griffiths, Anita N., "The WISC as a Diagnostic-Remedial Tool for Dyslexia," *Academic Therapy*, XII:4, 401-409.

7. Gur, R. E. and Gur, R. C., "Correlates of Conjugate Lateral Eye Movement in Man," Lateralization in the Nervous System, *Academic Press*, 1976.

8. Levy, Jerre and Reid, Marylou, "Variations in Writing Posture and Cerebral Organization," *Science* 194, 337-339.

9. Silverstein, Shel, "Where the Sidewalk Ends, the Poems and Drawings of Shel Silverstein," *Harper and Row*, New York, 1974, 58-59.

10. Witelson, Sandra, "Sex and the Single Hemisphere: Specialization of the Right Hemisphere for Spatial Processing," *Science*, July, 1976, 425-427.

HOW DYSLEXIA LOOKS

TO THE TEACHER

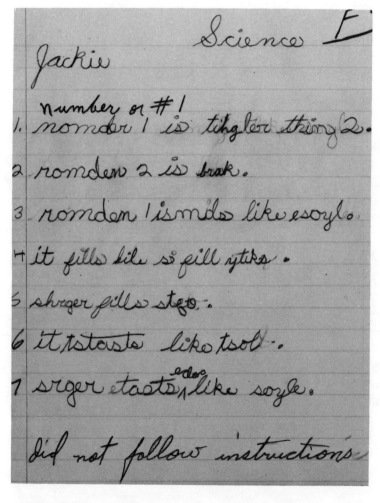

Jackie is twelve and has Very Superior intelligence as measured by the Wechsler Intelligence Scale for Children.

[Handwritten spelling test on lined paper]

Ray? You must learn how to make your cursive letters correctly!

1 thing   27 Dabk (black)
2 X cream m   28 X mant (next)
3 kill   29 nrene
4 well   30 X yaer (year)
5 dois   31 or
6 six   32 sent
7 ground   33 X ejangr
8 anove   34 X herir
9 doing   35 X huit
10 looking   36 X pelly
11 X pimping   37 around
12 please   38 X habaut (about)
13 should   39 X oud (owl) (low)
14 also   40 flower
15 X opne   41 X toun
16 waer   42 X low
17 X reinor   43 X thow
18 keep   44 X wineda
19 chair X chaerg   45 playing
20 clock   46 working
21 catck   47 eating
22 duck   48 walking
23 X stick   49 helping
24 X chickme   50 hunting
25 stick
26 X seanae

Ray is ten years old and is in second grade. He has High Average intelligence as measured by the Wechsler Intelligence Scale for Children.

Preparation for lesson: Joe was given a card with the word *brown* printed on it in brown. He was asked to use this card to copy the word until he thought he could spell it. He gave up trying to copy it in his notebook and tried to copy it on the card.

If you cannot read this, turn the page upside down and hold it up to a mirror.

126

F—

N1

of

I love Heres but riding
it is my favrit sports
be cause I love the stril
of thim not only be cause
of the dore but be cause
of the way he trus.

F

milissia   Feb. 3. 1977

Milissia, I can't read this.

E + G ++

THE AUTHOR

Anita N. Griffiths, EdD, is an educational counselor in private practice. Her professional experience includes fifteen years as a kindergarten and elementary school teacher, as well as college teaching positions. Dr. Griffiths has been an assistant professor of education at the University of South Florida (Tampa) and professor of psychology at Polk Community College (Winter Haven). She has published articles in professional journals such as the *Quarterly Journal* of the Florida Academy of Science, and *Academic Therapy*; and she has contributed a chapter to *Perspectives in Learning Disabilities.* She is a member of the American Psychological Association, the Florida Psychological Association, and the National Association for Children with Learning Disabilities. Dr. Griffiths lives and works in Lakeland, Florida.